A S

* L

Dress for excess.

* Be the other woman.

* Introduce him to your sex toys.

* Fed-Ex him your panties.

When you follow these rules, and the others in this book, you'll take control of both your relationship and your life. You'll be the aggressive, exotic, vocal woman you always knew you could be! And we'll guide you every step of the way. We'll be there when you're getting dressed, doing your make-up, deciding which sex toys to display on your coffee table....

The Other Rules are simple. And sexy. They're about gratification. Having the kind of fun you want now. Because nobody knows what's going to happen tomorrow. You might fall in love with Prince Charming and get married. And then where would you be? Spending the rest of your life wondering if maybe, just maybe, you should have sown a few more wild oats while you had the chance.

We don't want you to be stupid. Practice safe sex. Stay away from psychos. But forget sitting home alone on Saturday night because a man didn't call you by Wednesday. What's to keep you from calling him? Paging him? Showing up at his apartment wearing only high heels, Saran Wrap, and an old raincoat? *Nothing*!

For years, we have been following these rules, huskily whispering them to friends and lovers—sometimes one and the same. We know they work. We've proved it again and again. In a manner of days—or hours, if you're a quick learner—you'll know they work, too!

THE OTHER RULES

Never Wear Panties
On a First Date
and Other Tips

BY ANN BLAKELY
AND JULIA MOORE

First Masquerade Edition 1998

First Printing April 1998

ISBN 1-56333-658-8

Manufactured in the United States of America
Published by Masquerade Books, Inc.
801 Second Avenue
New York, N.Y. 10017

The authors wish to thank:

Aaron, Adam, Adrian, Alan, Alberto, Alden, Alexander, Alfredo, Angelo, Anthony, Aram, Archibald, Arlo, Arthur, Axel, Ben, Bobby, Bono, Bruno, Bryan, Byron, Caleb, Calvin, Carlos, Cesar, Chad, Charlie, Chico, Christian, Christopher, Claudio, Collin, Conrad, Corey, Craig, Dallas, Dameron, Damon, Daniel, Dashell, David, Dennis, Dirk, Douglas, Drew, Duff, Duncan, Edgar, Edmondo, Eduardo, Elliot, Emilio, Ernest, Evan, Ewan, Fabrice, Farlan, Fausto, Felipe, Fergus, Fidel, Forest, Francesco, Frank, Frankie, Fraser, Frederick, Gabino, Gabriel, Gael, Gavin, Graham, Grendel, Guiseppe, Guy, Hamilton, Hamlet, Hank, Hans, Hiram, Houston, Hunter, Ian, Isaac, Irwin, Ivan, Jacob, Jack, Jamie, Joe, Joel, John, Johnny, Jordan, Kaleb, Keith, Kent, Kirk, Lars, Leonard, Lew, Lloyd, Lou, Lucas, Luigi, Luke, Mack, Manfred, Mario, Mark, Matteo, Matthew, Michael, Mick, Miles, Milos, Morgan, Nathan, Nester, Norwell, Oded, Orion, Orlando, Ormond, Oscar, Otis, Owen, Oxford, Paolo, Paul, Parker, Pascal, Peter, Philip, Prescott, Quentin, Quinton, Rafael, Ramon, Raymond, Raul, Reed, Reid, Richard, Rico, Ripley, Roberto, Roman, Ronald, Ross, Roy, Royce, Ruben, Salvatore, Sam, Sancho, Sandy, Scott, Sean, Sergio, Seth, Shane, Sloan, Slim, Spencer, Stefano, Steven, Tavis, Taylor, Ted, Thad, Thomas, Tim, Todd, Tony, Tyler, Ugo, Uri, Valentino, Van, Vincenzio, Vito, Wade, Wallace, Walter, Welby, Whitby, Winston, Wolf, Xavier, Yago, and Zach.

Without their help—and the help of a few others whose names escape us at the moment (you know who you are!)—this book could never have been written.

The best way to hold a man is in your arms.

—*Mae West*

Contents

BONUS RULES FOR OVERACHIEVERS

A Note From the Authors
About *The Rules*

By now you've read (or at least heard about) *The Rules*, that moronic marriage manual that supposedly tells you everything you need to know about how to trap a man and drag him kicking and screaming to the altar. We're here to tell you that the two girls who wrote that book are wrong. They're not just wrong: They're dangerous. For some reason, these "must get married" maniacs are teaching women not to look at men, not to talk too much, not to call men up or call them back. (Which to us seems just plain rude.) These authors say that the man must be the aggressor and that the woman should be the pursued instead of the pursuer.

Based on extensive interviews, we have verified what

1

we already thought—that this advice couldn't be farther from the truth. Men want women to maintain clear and steady eye contact. Men like women who make the first move. They want them to return their phone calls. And we want to know what in the world makes these authors think that a man who likes a chase is going to stick around with a woman after he's caught her? If he's excited by a pursuit, won't he be pursuing some other woman next? His secretary, the baby-sitter, that cute ski instructor? That's just common sense.

To us the advice in this manipulative guide to groom-grabbing seems detrimental to women's mental health and self-respect. In our opinion, relationships should not be based on phony attitudes, but fun. If you can have fun with your date—be it by engaging in a little public fondling, dipping yourself into chocolate fondue, or finding out what happens to Saran Wrap when it gets wet—then life will be exciting and enjoyable. And there will be a lot less pressure on you to conform to somebody else's reality.

This is why we decided to write *The Other Rules*, the *real* way to find happiness and sexual bliss in your life-time. Our guide has little to do with getting married and everything to do with having a good time. In times of doubt (and we have very few of these), we like to remember Isadora Duncan's famous words of wisdom: "Any intelligent woman who reads the marriage contract, and then goes into it, deserves all the consequences."

P.S. If you are currently practicing the advice given in *The Rules*, we suggest that you call up all of your intelligent girlfriends and confess what you're doing. Tell your girlfriends that you've been trying out those "time-tested secrets for capturing the heart of Mr. Right," and let them plan an intervention. You may need to be thoroughly detoxed before our principles can work for you. It'll be embarrassing (not to mention time-consuming for all of you) but definitely worth it.

Things might feel scary at first. Life always is when you've been brainwashed. But everything will turn out okay. We promise. So erase the silly ideas those other women taught you and replace them with the correct concepts, which are clearly and carefully outlined in this book.

Chapter 1
The History of the Other Rules

No one is really sure where the Other Rules originated. Some say they were translated from the ancient Greek. Others believe they were written on slips of paper and tucked into fortune cookies. Ann's mother claims she learned them from her aunt Trudy, who picked them up from a mechanic named Bruno in the backseat of a 1957 Chevy. Julia's sister says they were spelled out on a Ouija board at a slumber party she went to in high school.

After some serious research, we realized that we discovered the Other Rules from our friend Fifi. And Fifi learned the Other Rules from her grandmother, Trixabelle, a French courtesan, who read them on a flyer she saw pasted in the ladies' room at the Eiffel Tower.

Back then, these rules were called "Les Autres Règles." However, under any name and in any language, the Other Rules made it possible for Trixabelle to work only half as long and half as hard as most French courtesans and make twice the money. Trixie almost kept the Other Rules to herself until her dying day, when beckoning to her bedside her favorite grand-daughter, Fifi, she finally divulged these fabulous bits of advice that had kept her in the black for so long.

In the beginning, Fifi was very hush-hush about the Other Rules. She was afraid if she revealed them some of her friends might have figured out she was having affairs with their husbands. But we watched her carefully and knew she had secrets to share. How else to explain the steady stream of handsome and debonair companions begging for a glimpse of her garters? After being tied up and tickled for sixteen hours straight, Fifi finally gave in and decided to reveal the Other Rules to us.

Needless to say, at first we were skeptical. Here we were, demure women, used to being the silent partners in our relationships. We rarely spoke to men, never looked them in the eye, and refused to let them realize that we were actually smarter than they were. It's how most of us had been taught to behave.

Within our hearts, we longed to be free to wink at guys. We wished we could cut our hair in short pixie styles like Jean Seberg or Twiggy. We had no desire to pick up after sloppy husbands, carpool the kids, or be den mothers. Forget the white wedding, the gown, the rehearsal dinner, and the honeymoon: We wanted to have fun, now! So, quietly, over chilled cosmopolitans and other exotic drinks at our favorite bars, or during kick-boxing lessons in downtown gyms, we passed along the Other Rules.

And the word began to spread!

Of course we've run into our share of Doubting Susans. Some women think the Other Rules were just made up. We understand. We felt that way, too, when we first got wind of these seductive secrets from Fifi. But after considering what life was like as the pretty adornment on the arm of some Neanderthal, we decided to give the concepts a whirl. And, wow, did they work!

Suddenly we were no longer wallflowers waiting for guys to come by and ask us to dance. We were doing the asking (and doing the dancing) on top of bars, tables, and the occasional stage. Our purses were filled with the phone numbers of eligible men. Our complexions took on the healthy glow that only a great sex life can achieve. After each earth-shaking evening, we promised to adhere even more closely to these wonderful words of wisdom.

Yes, we'll admit it. At first some of the rules struck us as odd. Still, when something works, you don't question why, you simply take another stiletto step forward. With our closest friends, we took these creative concepts to heart and became predatory tigresses, with dates every night of the week and most afternoons, too.

Pretty soon other women started asking us for advice. They said, "Ann and Julia, is there any way that we could be man-magnets like you?" Well, we weren't going to go the same route as Fifi. We don't like being on the receiving end of a tickling-'til-you-burst-session. But we didn't show our hand immediately.

We shared a few of the ideas: Rules 1 through 3, Rules 15 through 19, Rule 30. But we kept some secrets secret. Until we started realizing our friends were getting the Other Rules wrong! Instead of being bold and beautiful, they were sulking and silent. Instead of making direct eye contact, they refused to go outside, and they wore dark sunglasses indoors to avoid—Heaven forbid!—even accidentally looking at a guy. Instead of talking when they wanted to, calling men when they felt like it, and having sex at the *start* of every date, they were reverting to their old ways: never saying a word, refusing to answer the phone, and becoming frigid and withdrawn.

So we decided it was time to take action. And that is how the Other Rules were born.

Chapter 2
What Are the Other Rules?

The Other Rules are all about gratification. They're about dressing sexy, French kissing in public, and making love in the back row of a movie theater. The Other Rules are a simple set of secrets to becoming a more aggressive, flamboyant, and vocal you. If you follow the Other Rules, you're going to find that your world is suddenly a lot more dramatic. You will no longer be watching soap operas. You'll be living them.

Remember this: *Not all women are created equal.* Some women want one thing out of life: to get married. They don't really care whom they're married to, as long as they have that ring. Pathetic, isn't it? These women are insufferable bores. They would never consider masturbating in the ladies' room during their lunch hour. They don't own even one pair of crotchless panties. And they actually think there's something wrong with sleeping with a guy they never want to see again. They hold the promise of sex in front of a man as if it were a carrot on the end of a stick. And while many men may fall for it, this isn't the way Other Rules girls think.

When you practice the Other Rules, you will no longer be on the outskirts of society looking in. You'll be the one dancing on top of the bar (Rule 15). You'll be the girl in the Saran Wrap (Rule 9). You'll be the other woman (Rule 24).

We want to assure any skeptics that you won't have any problem practicing the Other Rules. They're easy. In simpler terms, you're easy. If you want to call him, call him. If you need to page him, page him. If you think his butt is divine, stare at it with your mouth open and lick your lips when he looks your way. If you do exactly what you feel like doing, you're practicing the Other Rules. If at any time you find yourself biting your tongue because you're afraid he won't like what you have to say, you're not practicing the Other Rules. Simple as that.

Of course, some critics may say that we're encouraging women to be, well, loose. That the Other Rules reduce men to sex objects. That we're suggesting that girls sleep with whomever they want to, whenever they want to, wherever they want to. That we're even encouraging women to keep extra condoms in their handbags in case they meet that special someone on the subway home. Sure we are. You got a problem with that?

Other critics might point out that sleeping around is simple. They might even ask: "Why would I need to read a book to tell me *that?*" To this we say, *The Other Rules* is filled with important and personally tested data! In this book, we'll explain exactly how to get his attention with one look alone. We'll describe what a pair of seamed stockings and stilettos can do for you. We'll walk you right through a successful first date—from what not to wear to what to serve for breakfast. We'll teach you how to give him a hard-on simply by pursing your lips, explain the importance of beating him at pool, and tell you the exact amount of time you should leave him handcuffed to your bed. These rules may sound extreme, but we promise you that we've tried them all and that they work!

But are we saying that you can *never* have a boyfriend? *Au contraire*, ladies. We're saying why stop at one? You can have as many as you want! You can have that winsome waiter at the café on the corner, the built bartender at your local pub, the handsome hunk stacking fruit at the grocery store. And moreover, why stop at men? You can try your hand, if you're so inclined, at a lesbian relationship. (After all, it's very chic at the moment.) Have them all, we say. Have them all!

If you're feeling fuzzy about any of this, don't worry. It will all become clearer once you read *The Other Rules*.

Read it over and over again. Commit it to memory. Get these rules tattooed on your body if necessary. Whenever you feel yourself backsliding—not calling that cute guy in Accounting, averting your eyes from the attractive pair of buns in front of you in line at the grocery store —reread *The Other Rules*. Create a support group of women who can help you get back on track if you find yourself slipping (more on this in the Appendix). Think about never being alone again! Not on any night of the week, any lunch hour, any coffee break! Think about great sex. Great sex that makes moving impossible afterward. You'll just lie there in the afterglow, your limbs entwined in his (or hers), and sigh your thanks to us.

What we're trying to tell you is something that other book doesn't want you to think about: You've only got one life, kiddo. Live it for pleasure. With our help, you'll find that a sexually satisfying social life is as easy as Fed-Exing your panties to the man of your dreams. But before you do that, turn the page.

Chapter 3
Meet an Other Rules Girl

Let's take a closer look at Fifi, the girl who divulged the Other Rules. Fifi is a gorgeous, world-traveling supermodel who has fabulously sexy hips. She's an ace poker-player who can beat any man at pool. She can say "I want you" in seventeen languages, and even without her contacts in, knows how to give a very good come-hither stare.

Believe us when we say that men flock to her. They sniff her out as if she were wearing a special perfume made from human pheromones. (Maybe she is!) If you're looking for Fifi at a party, you'll find her either merrily lap-dancing with an eligible bachelor or batting her eyelashes at the host's best friend. Because Fifi knows what she wants, and mostly she just wants to have fun.

And that's what the Other Rules are all about. Other Rules girls are the original good-time girls. Look at Fifi. She confidently approaches men she finds interesting. She talks first when she sees a guy she likes. She calls men in the middle of the night. She memorizes the layout of their homes and peers in their windows. Her life is exciting.

She has much more fun than her old-fashioned sisters sitting at home waiting for the right man to call, circling dance floors aimlessly in the hope that Mr. Right will notice them. "Why wait?" asks Fifi. "Get on the dance floor and shake your booty. Corner the guy you like in the elevator and pull the 'stop' button. Make tonight the night when chocolate syrup finally finds its rightful place in your bedroom routine."

When you find yourself near a Fifi, you may wonder what she's doing to attract men, aside from the fact that she's a gorgeous, lap-dancing supermodel. If you watch her closely, you'll realize that she's not doing anything specific to attract men. At least not intentionally. She's just being herself. And Fifi's self is one who likes to party, have sex, and take off her top in public. It's just the way she is. If men find that appealing, that's their prerogative.

During the aforementioned tickling session, when we tied Fifi to her bed and ran ostrich feathers over her naked body until she confessed the Other Rules, we were somewhat taken aback. Could we honestly be ourselves on a first date, as she assured us we could? Could we return calls from men and make direct eye contact? It all seemed so strange to us. So daring. So, shall we say, French. We were used to faking everything, from our smiles to our orgasms, but Fifi, through her hysterical laughter, shouted: "No!"

Fifi made everything seem so simple. She said to forget what our grandmothers told us, forget the fact that we still earned less pay than men did for equal work. Forget it all.

She gave us the real message, the honest truth: If you want to enjoy dating, treat men like you want to treat them. Treat them like they deserve to be treated. Stare at them. Stalk them. Make them call you "Mommy." They'll come panting at your feet, begging for more.

How *nouveau*, we thought to ourselves. How absolutely brilliant. We looked at Fifi, tied so beautifully to her bed, her well-manicured toes pointing to the ceiling, her body still shaking with the last of her helpless giggles. We wanted to be like Fifi, to have what she had: a pretty name, a full dance card, and earth-shaking sex every night of the week.

We decided to give her Other Rules a try. And—*Vive la France!*—our lives took a turn for the better.

THE OTHER RULES

Rule 1
Be a Vixen: Your Kitchen, Your Bedroom, Your Closet, and You!

For a woman, an upright life is the one that leads her to her grave practically unnoticed by anyone!
— COLETTE

Reread this rule. It says vixen, not virgin. If you had pulled a pair of white cotton panties out and were ready to step into them, you can put them back. (Or at least save them for later, when we discuss being a good girl on the outside and a bad girl on the inside. Which is, by the way, so much fun that we get a little shiver just thinking about it!)

Why would you want to be a vixen? Well, vixens are the epitome of Other Rules girls. Vixens are feminine and feline. Practical and predatory. Judicious and juicy. They know how to dress, how to shop, how to give a man a woody with one single look. They are the kind of women you should be looking up to. (And you'll *have* to. Vixens cruise the streets in high heels wherever they go.)

If you're not a vixen yet, have no fear. You'll be one by the end of this book! And we'll walk you through every step of the way. Because we know what it's like to want something. We were once just like you. And now we're making it our goal to help every luckless lady out there who wants to change her position in life—or at least, learn a few new ones.

Before we focus on you, let's take a good look at your apartment. How you keep your place could make the difference between being alone or with someone. So let's start in the kitchen. First, we want you to drastically rethink what you do in here. If you're only using your kitchen for cooking or eating—boring!—you're missing out on some incredibly sexy opportunities. Kitchens have countertops. They have sturdy tables. They have linoleum floors. The mind boggles at the possibilities!

Before you bring a man in here to play, let's check out the contents of your fridge. If you don't have the items we've listed for you below, then slide into something sultry, slip on a pair of fishnet stockings and high-heeled slingbacks, and head over to the grocery store. (We hear that's a pretty good place to meet new men....)

<u>WHAT TO KEEP IN YOUR FRIDGE</u>

Champagne

Ice

Oysters

Chocolate syrup

Creamed corn (*buy in bulk*)

That's it!

<u>WHAT HE SHOULD NEVER FIND IN YOUR FRIDGE</u>

Lite beer (*it gives men hives*)

Prunes

Chicken livers

Onions

Fruit roll-ups

Carob anything

Tofu

Slimfast

When you live the life of a vixen, you're not going to be thinking about food: You're going to hungry for something else entirely. In fact, you will probably find that the Other Rules way of life is the simplest and most fun way to lose weight in the world. (For more on this, look at the "Aphrodisiacs Diet" outlined in the Appendix, in which we help you understand how your chocolate craving could be more easily satisfied by fabulous orgasms.) And think about it: If you do get famished (since sex does burn off plenty of calories), you'll send out for sushi or grilled veggies on foccacia or something.

If you're one of those practical types who simply *must* have food in her apartment, stock up on chocolate syrup, whipped cream, strawberries, chopped nuts, molasses, maple syrup, and honey. Sure, these may seem calorie-rich, but you won't be eating much of them. *He* will. Here's how the game goes: You'll be the starting point for a sundae. One that he'll enjoy finishing every last drop of. Occasionally, you can let him be the basin for the sundae toppings, but we'll bet that you'll wind up sliding around in more syrup than you lick up. Believe us, these types of foods make both the prep and the clean-up a lot of fun.

What about real food, you say? Heaven forbid! Other Rules girls never cook. Never! Look, ladies, we don't even know how to boil water. Why should we? There are a million restaurants out there and a million men who will take you to them. The most chef-like exertions you'll be making at home are filling your tub with chocolate pudding or decorating his private parts with whipped cream and butterscotch topping. Cooking, in our opinion, is a total waste of time. Of course, this shouldn't stop you from buying that cute little black vinyl apron you saw in *The Sinful Chef* catalog. (We have one, too.)

And while we're on the subject of things Other Rules girl never do, let's not forget laundry. Or, rather, let's forget about it completely. Never, ever, do his laundry! Please. You have better things to do with your time, like painting your toenails a glorious shade of neon blue, or buffing the dead skin off your elbows and heels. Other Rules girls do not do chores for men. We may dress up as naughty French maids in very tiny black uniforms; we may slide into shoulder-length rubber gloves and hose him down with a shower nozzle. But remember, pretending to clean and *actually* cleaning are two entirely different things! If you ever forget our advice, just say this Jerry Hall quote out loud to yourself: "My mother said it was simple to keep a man; you must be a maid in the living room, a cook in the kitchen, and a whore in the bedroom. I said I'd hire the other two and take care of the bedroom bit."

That said, let's move to the bathroom. Every Other Rules girl we've met spends a lot of time in the bathroom. Primping. Prepping. Posing. And lest you think we're slipping, bathrooms are also fun places to play with your mate. Take a shower together. Wash each other's hair. Take a bubble bath. Shave each other bare (a really sexy treat). So check your supplies. You should have at least one of each of the following:

WHAT TO KEEP IN YOUR BATHROOM	WHAT HE SHOULD NEVER FIND IN YOUR BATHROOM
Bubble bath (scented)	Acne medication
Baby oil	Depilatories
Candles	Douche
Shower soap	FDS
Loofah	Maxi-pads
Long-handled brushes	A pregnancy test kit
A fluffy bath mat	Antifungal cream
A box of condoms	Tweezers

Time to focus our scrutiny on your bedroom. We know you may think that mood lighting hides anything, but we like to play with the lights on, too. (And most men appreciate this!) This means that your bedroom should be a properly outfitted place to play. Go pick up mirrors for your ceiling, cash in your 401K for a bearskin rug, exchange your plain light bulbs for red ones, and get ready to redo your boudoir.

If you are a true vixen, you'll know that the bed won't be used nearly as often as the living room floor, love seat, or porch swing, but that doesn't mean you should be sleeping on the same futon you've had since college. Your bed should reflect your classy yet practical side. Personally, we prefer a four-poster bed, or one with well-made brass head- and footboards (more on this later). You should also choose a good, sturdy mattress. You don't want any squeaky springs, especially if you live with roommates who'll make fun of you.

If you decorate your bed as we suggest below, we can promise you this: he'll always have a place in his, um, heart for you.

WHAT TO HAVE ON YOUR BED	WHAT NOT TO HAVE ON YOUR BED
Satin sheets	Stuffed animals
At least two pillows	A live animal (*Men hate cats. If you have one, say good-bye!*)
	Your ex

Let's move to your closet. Aside from men, the most important thing to an Other Rules girl is her clothes. How you look is extremely important. To make it simple for you, we've created an alphabetized list. Believe us when we say that it's absolutely mandatory for you to have at least one representative item from each letter below. If you don't, then please, please get yourself up to speed. (You'll notice, if you're a clever girl, that some of the items listed are fabrics or materials, not actual apparel. In this case, choose an article of clothing that's tight, sexy, and made from the suggested material.)

The ABCs of sexy dressing

Anklet, Apron, Angora Sweater

Bustier, Bikini, Blindfold

Catsuit, Corset, Crotchless Panties, Crisco

Dog Collar, Doctor's Stethoscope, Diamonds

Earrings, Edible Panties, Exotic Dancer's Outfit

Fishnets, Feather Boa, French Maid Outfit

G-string, Garters, Go-Go Boots

High Heels, Handcuffs, Harem-Girl Outfit

Indian Sari, Iridescent Scarf, Indecent anything

Jeans (*ripped, tight*), Jumper, Jock Strap (*for cross-dressers*)

Knickers, Kilt, K-Y

Leather, Lace, Leopard, Liquid Latex

Merry Widow, Masking Tape, Mermaid Outfit

Nurse's Uniform, Nightie, Nipple Clamps

Opera Gloves, Ostrich Feathers

Pearls, Peignoir, Plastic Wrap

Queen's Crown, Quirt

Rubber Raincoat, Rope, Riding Crop

Stockings, Satin, Slip

Thong, Thigh-Highs, Tattoo

Underwear, Underwater Gear, Underwire Bra

Velvet, Velour, Vinyl

White Cotton Panties, Wrapping Paper,

Wonder Woman Outfit (*with cape*)

X-rated Anything

Your Birthday Suit

Zippered Skirt, Zippered Dress, Zippered Boots

<u>CLOTHES AN OTHER RULES GIRL WOULD NEVER WEAR</u>

Anything with epaulets or shoulder pads
Anything baggy or "grunge"
Anything knee-length
Anything with an elastic waistband
Sweats
The ripped flannel robe you've had since high school
Panties

Now you know your ABCs. Next time you'll get dressed with ease!

What about your regular clothes, you say? Well, it's easy. As any personal shopper worth her salt will tell you, before you get dressed, it's important to determine your "season." Once you know which season you are, you'll have a much easier time both dressing and shopping! But we're not recommending that you actually seek out a consultant on this: She'll only charge you $400 while she drapes fabric over your shoulders and makes "tsk, tsk" noises with her tongue. We can help you right now. For free. Just answer the following questions:

Were you born in the spring? Then it's mandatory for you to wear at least one piece of clothing with a floral pattern every day. You may include your bra on this.

Is your birthday in the autumn? We recommend wearing gold-toned clothing, or dresses the color of falling leaves, or made from fallen leaves.

Were you born in the winter? Make sure that you're

wearing something fur! At all times. (If you are anti-fur, then wear a ski suit.)

Are you a summer baby? Then by all means, doll face, put on your bikini!

Our other dressing advice centers on staying ahead of the trends. Buy *all* the European fashion magazines you can afford. (We know they can run $10 an issue, but they're worth it! Skip the bagel from the café on the corner—too many calories, anyway. Have an English muffin at home instead, and you'll be able to squeeze in at least one Italian *Vogue* a month. Plus you might be able to squeeze into a smaller pair of jeans!)

European fashion magazines are always filled with sexier clothing than their American counterparts. (We have a copy of the French *Elle* that is literally dedicated to the "les fesses," or "the buttocks," which explains exactly how to dress to show off that part of your anatomy!) Also, since European fashion magazines seem to pick up on the fashion rage one or two seasons ahead of time you'll be prancing around looking extremely cutting-edge, and two years from now your friends will be commenting on how hip you've looked all this time!

Once you are dressed you need to accessorize. You may have heard the advice that after you get dressed, you should look in the mirror and then remove the most obvious item that you see—perhaps a neon scarf or a weighted-down charm bracelet. Well, our more modern approach to this rule is to stare in the mirror and make sure you are wearing at least *one* obvious item. Something spangled. Something sequined. Something sparkly. If you're not, then go get one. Quickly! How will men find you if they don't notice you in the first place?

We've been avoiding this—self-appraisal is *sooo* difficult—but it's time to take a look at you. Yes, *you*. Stand in front of a mirror and give yourself a good once-over. Are you at least 5'7"? No? Poor baby! You should be. No less an authority than *Glamour* suggests that a "gorgeous" woman is at least that tall: apparently, men like a woman to come up to about shoulder-high. If you don't measure up, go out this very instant and buy a pair of heels that make you 5'7"! Otherwise we simply don't have anything else to say to you: you might as well just call it quits as far as dating goes. (Need help doing the math? If you're 5'4", get 3" heels. If you're 4'7", you'll need ten-inchers, available, thank God, at Frederick's of Hollywood. If you're *under* 4'6", you're too young to be reading this book. Go put it back in your sister's room and *stop snooping*!)

Time to analyze your hair. Are you a blonde? Brunette? Redhead? Great! Men love all three. And as long as you're not all three at once, there's no problem. And if you're at a funky stage of your life, and your hair is currently blue or green or purple or yellow or skunk-striped, well, we're okay with that, too. (Although we're wondering what kind of job you have.) Don't worry about the length, for God's sake. Look, as long as you *have* hair, you're fine. Or, if you're bald, but really,

really pretty, like that babe in the first *Star Trek* movie, you'll do fabulous, too. At least, with Trekkies. (And from what we can tell, there are an awful lot of them out there!)

How's your vision? Do you wear glasses? Do you *have* to? Are you legally blind without them? We hate to bring this up, but everybody knows that men don't make passes at girls who wear glasses. You must have heard that from your mother or your grandmother, and we have to admit that in this case, she spoke the truth. Even if you're the one who's going to be making the passes, it doesn't hurt to go get yourself some contacts. (An exception to this rule is if you can carry off that sexually repressed librarian thing, where you shake out your hair, take off your glasses, and *voilà*! You're an unbelievably stunning—yes, you guessed it—vixen! If you can do that, by all means, wear your glasses, four-eyes. We're in awe.)

Let's look at your body. Are you double-jointed? If so, give yourself ten extra points for each double-joint, triple points if you have double-jointed hips. (Yes, we're keeping score. Weren't you?) Do you have any freckles? Men think freckles are sexy, especially tiny golden ones on the bridge of the nose. Were you blessed with pretty feet? Thank your parents! There are many foot-fetishists out there who will love to kiss each one of your adorable little toes! (And some who will actually pay you money to buy your used shoes!) Men especially like toes that are well-polished a deep, shiny red.

We personally like Revlon's "Cherries in the Snow."

It's time to talk bust size. (We know you were dreading it, but we're all friends here, right? We can be honest with each other.) If you are unlucky in the cleavage department—meaning that you're smaller than a 36CC —we recommend that you either invest in a WonderBra or move to France. Unlike American men, who are obsessed with cleavage, French men have a thing for small-breasted women. They believe (bless their little hearts) that if you have breasts that would spill out of a champagne glass (saucer-style), you have too much. Isn't that darling? However, if you can't afford to move to Paris at the moment, you can trick American men into thinking you're more endowed than you are by dusting blush between your breasts to enhance the cleavage you've got. Because it's important to flaunt what you've got when you're an Other Rules girl!

Finally, write down your name. Look at it. Is it fun to say out loud? Is it frilly? Does it end with an -i, an -ie or a -y? It should! Other Rules girls all have names like Tiffany, Stefanie, Trixie, Corki, and Fifi. These kinds of names are fun for a man to say. They'll roll off his lips easily, especially during passionate moments. Plus, there's much less of a chance that he'll get your name wrong if at least half of it is the same as the names of all of his former lovers! We're right. You know we are. Visualize the handsome hunk of your dreams tied down to your four-poster bed (we told you it would come in handy) screaming, "Yes, Lacey, yesss!" Now imagine him saying:

"Yes, Mildred, yes…" Doesn't work quite as well, does it?

If that's not enough reason for you, think of some of the sexiest girls in history:

Traci Lords	Barbie Benton
Mamie Van Doren	Bettie Page
Christie Brinkley	Pussy Galore
Betty Boop	Cindy Crawford
Gypsy Rose Lee	Miss Piggy

If you have any problems choosing a new name, think of a fruit, like Cherry (that's the only one we could think of); or a dessert, like Candy or Taffy or Toffee or Cookie; or a beverage, like Brandy or Sherry.

What if you're a professional woman? Maybe you're a lawyer, or an accountant, or a financial analyst. There's no way on earth that you want some foo-foo, girlie name on your business card, right? You'd be the laughing stock of your office! Well, you can always choose a name that works two ways, one for work and one for play:

NAME:	NICKNAME:	NAME:	NICKNAME:
Alana	Lili	Margaret	Marti
Ann	Annie	Megan	Maggie
Barbara	Barbie	Roberta	Bobbi
Eleanor	Nelly	Samantha	Sami
Elizabeth	Libby	Sarah	Sally
Jean	Jeanie	Susan	Susie
Jennifer	Jenny	Victoria	Tori
Kristin	Kristie		

Of course, there are some perfectly fine, sexy names that don't end with -i, -ie, or -y. A partial list includes: Amber, Cecilia, Donna, Emerald, Ginger, Gloria, Layla, Lola, Marlena, Pamela, Pepper, Roxanne, Sugar, or Veronica. If your name has been immortalized in either a rock song or a sexy book, or adopted by an outrageous porn star, you're a winner by association. If your name is a spice or a precious gem, you're also doing fine. So you go, girl!

But some names simply must be changed. They must, we tell you, they must! These names include: Olga, Bertha, Harriet, Helga, and Mabel. We hate to say it, but try to avoid anything that sounds fat. We're not implying that *you're* fat (we'd *never* say that—at least, not to your face!), we're just being honest and telling you the image that your name conjures. And the image it conjures is of an overstuffed Swiss maid with thick wrists and arms.

If you don't believe anything else we say in this book, trust us on this: You will not get the handsome hunk of your dreams if your name evokes visions of a big-boned broad. When your new man tells his friends he's going out with Bertha, they'll roll their eyes and laugh. And that will be it.

So do the right thing. March down to the nearest courthouse (as quickly as you can march in your brand-new stilettos—it will get easier with practice, we promise), and change your name legally. You'll be glad you did!

Rule 2
Never Wear Panties On a First Date (and Other Helpful Hints)

> You never get a second chance to make a first impression. —WILL ROGERS

Let us explain. We're assuming that this is a first date, not a blind date. And we're also assuming that you have done your homework. You've scoped this man out completely —on the Internet, with a private detective, however you personally prefer to get your inside information. You know his background, his middle name, his dog's name, his grade point average, whether he's ever been with a man before, and so on. And you're still willing to go out with him. The lucky stiff.

Well, to us that means that you expect more from him than a salad, a movie, and a peck on the cheek good night. (And this, by the way, is not what you should be

doing on *any* date. If you need help choosing activities
—or positions—turn to Rule 8, Creamed Corn Wrestling
and Other Activities for a Slow Date.) Look, be honest.
It's us here. If you didn't have any romantic interest in
the guy, you'd have canceled the date and made plans to
go bar-hopping, *and* man-hunting, with your favorite,
frisky girlfriends.

But you didn't cancel. And you *do* like him. So now's
the time to ditch the undies. Yes, now. We're waiting!
Going pantyless accomplishes several very important
things. First, you're instantly assured that you are going
to feel wicked all night long. And wicked is very sexy.
You'll give yourself a mini-thrill whenever you cross or
uncross your legs, whenever a sudden gush of air ruffles
the panels of your dress, and when every man you walk
by does a double take. Second, if you do decide to sleep
with your date, he's going to think you're the coolest girl
on the planet. (Unless he's already dated an Other Rules
girl. In which case he simply won't believe his run of
good luck.) Third, you're not going to lose your under-
pants in some back alley again or have yet another good
pair torn off of you in a moment of heated passion.
Panties can be insanely expensive. Especially the nice
ones. Sure, you're going to parade around in your laciest
(and raciest) lingerie for him later. But not tonight.

Choose your best garters and stockings. (Fire-engine
red satin ones will win you extra points.) Put on your
favorite dress—the tighter the better. As far as fabric is
concerned, anything semi-sheer is nice if you're going

without panties. Slide into your heels. And let the breeze tickle your...fancy.

We want to be clear on something else. Just because you're not wearing panties doesn't mean he is a shoe-in to the bedroom (sofa, kitchen table, backseat, bathtub). You have every right *not* to sleep with him, no matter what you said on the phone, or how explicit your inter-office e-mail was, or what his friends told him about you. But if your date is moving along successfully—he likes you (and why shouldn't he?) and you're into him— you can easily turn up the heat by giving him access to the pantyless you. Start slowly. Flash a bit of your garters when you get out of the car. Rub against him while you're waiting in line to get into the club. Stand directly over a grate and do your best Marilyn Monroe (in *The Seven Year Itch*) impression. You get the idea.

Suppose you've been a good girl all your life and you find yourself thinking: "I just can't go without my undies." Maybe your mother was one of those who instructed you always to wear clean undies in case you got hit by a bus. (May we say that we've never quite understood the point of that advice? If you do get hit by a bus, are you really going to care who sees what?)

In any case, we have three words for you: practice, practice, practice. Walk around your apartment in the buff. Have completely naked weekends, when you don't wear a stitch of clothing for forty-eight hours. (Unless you're going out to get the mail; in that case, we'll allow you to slide into your robe.) Or try this: Sneak into the bathroom the next time you go to the mall! In short, whenever you have a free moment, take your panties off! Soon you'll feel completely at ease.

But even if after strolling around your place in the buff, you truly don't feel comfortable without your knickers on, we advise you to try crotchless panties. They will make you feel as if you're covered when you're really still bare down there. (Basically, you'll be fooling yourself!) And they're very sexy. Or better yet, wear edible panties, and offer to be his dessert. (Bonus: no need to launder them—they're a one-time deal.)

Another word of advice: Just because you go panty-less does not mean you should be letting it all hang out up top. Bras are still a must, unless you're either an AA cup, or simply naturally perky, in which case, we're envious beyond belief. If you're not either one of those, put on your nicest bra. *Not* one of the chewed-on looking bras you keep at the back of your drawer. In fact, throw those out right now. (Even if you don't have a date, you should be dressing nice for yourself! You're worth it.)

But why wear a bra, you say? If you're going to be bare below, shouldn't you go bare all the way? Won't your date find this even more exciting than the fact that you have no panties on? Nope. Guys like bras. Even if they fumble with them, unsure of whether the opening's in front or back—will they *never* learn?—men enjoy the feeling of releasing you. It's part of the game. And this *is* a game. One that, with our help, you're gonna win. And that's all that really matters, right?

Rule 3
Who to Date and Where to Find Him

I'm fond of anything that comes out of the sea—
and that includes sailors.
—JANET FLANNER

Let's say that you haven't actually gotten a date yet. You're still on the lookout, and you need our help. Hey, that's what we're here for. And in the next few chapters we're going to tell you exactly how to meet the man of your dreams, or at least the man of the moment. But before we explain the proper way to look at him, talk to him, and make him crazy, you need to find him. Or them. So refer to this handy-dandy chart below.

WHO THE BOYS ARE	WHERE THE BOYS ARE
• Actor: A guy who can role-play	*Local theater company*
• Ballplayer: A guy who can swing his bat	*Field near your house*
• Bodybuilder: A guy with one big muscle	*Gym (wear your lycra)*
• Baker: A guy with nice buns	*Pastry shop*
• Bartender: A guy with a fuzzy navel	*Bar*
• Chef: A guy with a thick rolling pin	*Your favorite restaurant*
• Cop: A guy with a big nightstick	*The highway (try speeding)*
• Cowboy: A guy with chaps and spurs	*Texas*
• Doctor: A guy with rubber gloves	*The clinic (fake a cough)*
• Electrician: A guy with a live wire	*Your house (jam the fuse box)*
• Farmer: A guy who looks good in overalls	*Corn field*
• Firefighter: A guy with a big hose	*Burn him up with a hot red dress*
• Fisherman: A guy with a long pole	*Rivers or streams (be the bait)*
• Flautist: A guy who can play his flute	*Orchestra pit*

WHO THE BOYS ARE	WHERE THE BOYS ARE
• Gardener: A guy who can trim your bush	*Botanical gardens*
• Knight: A guy with a long sword	*At a round table*
• Magician: A guy with a magic wand	*Kid's birthday party*
• Math teacher: A guy who knows his figures	*School*
• Mechanic: A real one	*The garage (sabotage your car)*
• Musician: A guy with rhythm	*Your favorite club*
• Pirate: A guy after buried treasure	*At sea*
• Plumber: A guy with a good wrench	*Under your sink*
• Pool player: A guy with a sharp stick	*Any local bar*
• Sailor: A guy who knows fore from aft	*Aboard ship*
• Shrink: A guy with a nice couch	*(Don't reveal the Other Rules!)*
• Surfer: A guy who can go tubular	*Hawaii*
• Tailor: A guy with nimble fingers	*Tailor shop (rip your clothes)*
• Waiter: A guy who knows your favorite "specials"	*Your favorite café*

Rule 4
The Stare—How to Let Him Know You Want Him

Any girl can be glamorous. All you have to do is stand still and look stupid.   —Hedy Lamarr

With the help of our fabulous list of places to meet men, you have actually found a guy you're interested in (or several guys you're interested in). So what do you do now, cupcake? You listen to us. (You should always be listening to us!) We're going to explain how to give a guy a meaningful look (several, actually), pass him a note, find out which car is his (so you can stick your number under his windshield wiper), track down where he launders his clothes (so you can slip one of your pretty G-strings into his package.) (More of these in the next chapter.)

Say that you see a handsome him across a crowded room. At a party, club, or gym, or even at work. You look at him and he looks back at you. How do you let him know you're interested without taking one step forward?

You stare.

We're not talking about engaging in one of those silly, juvenile contests to see which one of you can keep from blinking first. We're talking about making love to him with your eyes, and your eyes only.

Before we proceed, we want to make you feel comfortable with "the stare." You see, we know of at least one popular self-help book that will tell you not to look at guys. To let guys look at you instead. But how will you know he's looking at you if you're not looking at him, too? (You don't have eyes in the back of your head!) And how will he know that you're interested if you're busy taking in "the world in general," rather than his fine body in those tight jeans? We don't understand this book and others like it: They're confusing us and give us pounding headaches.

We'll start with one of our favorite stares, specifically, the "Look, Look Away, Look Back, Look Away," otherwise known as the "I Want You, Babe." In your repertoire of stares, this will be one you'll return to again and again. Why? Because we said so. And also because it works.

Before we start, you'll need to go get a hand mirror. Yes, we'll wait. Ready? Now look at yourself. You're stunning, you know that? What we'd do to have lips like those! Okay, now get ready. We're going to teach you the stare. Read the following directions carefully. Then practice them in the mirror.

First, look directly into your eyes.

Now, lower your chin and look up. Think ingenue. Think coy. Think Lolita.

Next, look down, and sort of to the right, as if there's a naked picture of Brad Pitt on the floor that you can barely see out of the corner of your eye. (Don't turn all the way around looking for it! We're using this as an example.)

Okay, now forget Brad and look back up. (*Forget him*, we said.)

Now, down again. There's Brad's butt!

Perfect.

This is the stare of all stares. It achieves several very important things simultaneously. First, you make eye contact. *Direct* eye contact. Which, we assure you, is very sexy! Second, you appear shy and vulnerable. (*Appear* is the key word. This is all one great act. But men eat this up. We don't know why. They just do.) When you look back at him, you're saying, "Nope. Not so shy after all." (Men love *this* even more. It confuses them and makes them all hot and bothered.) Then you look away again, letting him know that you can live without him. You already *do* live without him. And he would be lucky if you'd even deign to look at him again.

Practice this in the mirror while we go get ourselves

another cappuccino. When we get back, we expect you to be a pro.

Ready? Now we'll move on to what we call the "Kitty-Cat Eyelash Bat." This is a winner! It works for us every time! For this particular move, we're going to a book written by an animal expert who tells us that when cats bat their eyes slowly (open, close, open) they are actually giving their owners a kiss. They're saying, in their own friendly feline way: "I'm comfortable enough with you to close my eyes in front of you." This is what you want to do with the object of your affection. Kiss him with your eyelashes. (Don't stand so close that your lashes actually brush his skin. Save this for later when you're sitting in the back row of a movie theater.) For now, just look over at him, let him see you looking, then slowly close and open your eyes. It helps if you breathe in deeply when you do this. (Think yoga: Inhale through your nose when you close your eyes, exhale through your nose when you open them.) Act as if you just had the most devilish, delicious, or dangerous thought about him. Put some serious sparkle in your eyes when you look back at him. (Do this by thinking about smiling without actually smiling.)

You'll need to practice this look with a male friend. Otherwise you won't be able to judge very well for yourself if it's working, since your eyes will be closed during the most important step. Continue with the look until your friend gets a little bit uncomfortable. Once he starts squirming on the couch and asks you to please stop unless you're prepared to compromise your friendship, you know you're doing it right! And are we proud, by the way.

Now that you've mastered the two essential stares, we'll take a little break and work on your pout. Pouting is an art form. It makes you look very sexy in the style of a '20s movie star. This is easy. Simply think of a time when you didn't get something you wanted. Presto! That's all you need. Look in the mirror to make sure you're doing it right. Your bottom lip should be slightly plumped up and your eyes should have a glimmer of sadness in them. This is a look to give a guy who hasn't immediately found his way to your side. Your pout should make him want to help you, to fix what's troubling your itsy-bitsy little heart. It's what we like to call the "Precious Pout" or the "Well, What Are You Waiting For?"

It's time to move onto the final stare, which is a more difficult one, but we're sure you can handle it! This is called the "Eyelash Flutter," or the "I'm Coming! Yes! Now!!!!" First, take a deep breath through your nose, all the way up from your diaphragm. Now let your breath out in a rush through your mouth. Make it sound a bit shaky. You want to portray that you're having a difficult time controlling yourself. Clench your thighs together. Practice squeezing and releasing those inner muscles you use when you're trying not to pee. Once you get yourself good and worked up, add the I Want You, Babe stare. Ready? Flutter your lashes. Quickly!

Think hummingbird in midflight. Do the two together. On the subway. He'll either move far, far away from you or much closer to you. But, in all honesty, if you keep squeezing those muscles, you actually might not need him anymore. You decide.

Okay, big girl, you've graduated. It's time for you to move on to the more advanced attention getter in Rule 5, Leaving a Note to Get Noticed.

We'll be there in a minute. We're just going to do the Eyelash Flutter a few more times. For good measure.

Rule 5
Leaving a Note to Get Noticed

Sealed with a lick, 'cos a kiss wouldn't stick.
— ANONYMOUS

If the object of your attention is someone you know by sight, perhaps a man in your apartment building, office, or gym, then this will be a piece of cake. Watch him carefully the next time he goes to his car. You can try to time your schedule so that you're leaving at the same time he does. (Hang out at the gym until you understand his schedule, or ask your girlfriends in the office to help you keep tabs on him.) Do not let him get a good look at you, but follow him as closely as possible.

Pay attention to which car he gets into. So many cars look alike these days, you may want to note any distinguishing characteristics—bumper stickers, dents, and so on. (Make absolutely certain that you know which car is his! You don't want to slide an erotic message under a windshield wiper that turns out to belong to that geek in Personnel, do you?)

Next we want you to write him a note. Think back to high school if you need inspiration. If you weren't a note-passer, just pen a short little scribble in your best handwriting explaining that you think he's cute. (Of course you can improvise here. Say that you've noticed his abs, if he's a fellow aerobics fiend from your gym. Or that he looks hot in a tie, if you are a coworker. Or that you think he's got dreamy bedroom eyes or a fantastic smile that makes you quiver.) Sign it with a lipsticked kiss and put it under his windshield on a Friday. (Do not sign your name!)

On the next Friday (and not one day before), write him another note. This one can be more explicit. (Tell him you'd like to see his tie tied around your wrists, or that you think that a body as strong as his should be oiled up and put on display.) Seal this note with another kiss...and your initials.

On the third Friday, he's going to be expecting you. We're guessing he'll be waiting by his car, and if he's anything like the guys we've dated, he'll have roses in both hands. He'll be leaning against the hood of his car and smiling at you. This time, you can leave that kiss directly on his lips.

If you're after a boy you don't know, however—say,

someone you've seen in line at the dry cleaners—you're going to have a more difficult time. That's just the way it is, cutie. But don't worry: we're here to help. First, you need to be prepared to sweet-talk the person behind the counter. Explain that you're interested in the client who was just in, and find out if they will slip a note with your number into his clothes when he comes to pick them up. You're not really doing anything illegal, after all. If the dry cleaner is amenable (and if you've been your adorable self, he should be!), write a note and seal it in an envelope. (We do *not* recommend lipstick this time, since the man you're after just got his clothes cleaned.) Have the dry cleaner put the note on top of the laundered clothing.

If the apple of your eye goes to the laundromat instead of the dry cleaners, you will have a much easier time. After the first occasion in which your paths cross, try to find out his schedule—assign your girlfriends each a different laundry night. He's got to come back eventually! And then work your magic. Choose a washing machine right next to his. Smile seductively as you load in each one of your fancy undergarments. If you're a true Other Rules girl, we're guessing you'll be able to get some frilly article of clothing mixed in with his on your first night of laundry duty. Believe us, he'll be intrigued.

(Note: Simply because you took your clothes to the laundromat does *not* mean that you're breaking our rule about doing laundry! So don't worry your pretty little head, baby doll. You have to go through many trials and tribulations to meet a guy; you may even have to throw a load of laundry into the washing machine every once in awhile. Just don't make a habit of it!)

What about a total stranger? Let's say that someone who passes by you on the street makes your heart do a flip-flop. In this case, you're going to have to do some serious stalking. Follow the object of your affections as he goes on his merry way; hide in doorways or behind parked cars whenever he turns around. When he gets into a car, scribble down his license plate number. You can do a check through the DMV to get his name and address. (If they no longer give this information in your town, you may need to hire a P.I., who will surely be able to get you the information you need.) Once you have the address, drive to his house and proceed with the original "note" plan. If he doesn't call the police, you're in!

Rule 6
It Takes Two to Tango—
Asking Him to Dance

I'm saving the bass player for Omaha.
—JANIS JOPLIN

We *hated* dances in high school. The noise. The sweat. The dorks. We usually sat up in the bleachers and drank rum and coke smuggled into the gym in our thermoses. But if there had been any guys in our high school worth dancing with, then let us make one thing very clear: *We would have asked them to dance!*

Really. No way on earth that we would have sat on the sidelines and waited wimpily for some loser to ask us. Now it turns out that we didn't have to. Because there are dance clubs, raves, and concerts for us to go to where we can relive those high school days. And from the looks of things, dancing today is just what dancing always was. Which is why we preferred the bleachers all along. You can watch the other people making fools out of themselves. You can point and laugh. And you never have to move your feet, which, when you're wearing 10" platforms, is a true pleasure.

But if you really, really want to dance, and if you won't settle for wiggling that cute little booty of yours to the hep sounds of The Squirrel Nut Zippers in front of your bedroom mirror, then we'll give you some tips.

First, make sure you know what you're doing. Don't try to get by with the dance steps you did twenty years ago. Forget the electric slide. The bus stop. The shuffle. Don't even think of doing the mashed potato or the swim! If you need help figuring out how to shake your money maker, go to a dance club and watch the teenagers grooving. Kids always know what's in and what's out—way before adults catch on! Or watch videos on MTV. Often, you'll be able to pick up a few cool steps, even if you can't keep up with all the different moves. (We like Will Smith's "Getting Jiggy With It." Hell, we just like Will Smith.)

Next, know your music. Program your radio to pick up every good station in town. Listen carefully. We want you to feel the beat. To hear the beat. To live the beat. It's hard enough moving your feet without stomping all over his. Make it easier by learning the music ahead of time. Even if you don't like it. Even if you think Chumbawamba is a silly name for a group. Memorize every line.

Once you're familiar with the tunes, it's time to practice. (Think *The Full Monty* as an example of just what practice can do for totally uncoordinated klutzes!) First, get a mirror. Second, dance in front of it. See that stupid little "dancing face" you put on? Stop it! Right now! You look imbecilic! If you want to be a good dancer, you need to create a sexy dancing face. We think the best look is sort of a faraway gaze, as if your body is physically on the dance floor but your mind is in bed with Matt Dillon. (Exactly where *our* minds are most of the time!) Thinking about the marvelous Matt should give you the appropriate come-hither look, and it will also take your focus off your killer heels. Fantasizing about sex will also make your body looser and more relaxed. And pretty soon your partner won't want to dance anymore, and you two can go somewhere else where you can get off your feet. And onto your back.

Finally, never go to a line-dancing bar. Never ever. Sure, line-dancing looks like fun on the Country Cable Channel. But so does calf-wrestling. And what a mistake that was! Let us tell you!

Now you need to actually ask a guy to dance. We think the best way to do this is to bring a guy you like to a place where people dance, rather than simply showing up and having to scan the crowd for something decent that walks upright. If you do ask someone you know to accompany you to a club, please remember to be specific! Let him know he's about to go on a date! For example, do not say that you're going to a dance club and ask the object of your desire if he "needs a ride." He may go with you in order to meet other girls! (This actually happened to a friend of ours once, but in reverse. A guy asked her if she'd like a ride to their office party. She didn't know he meant they were going as a couple. As the night progressed, he found her out on the balcony with her hand on the crotch of a young art assistant. "Is this how you usually behave on a date?" he asked. "I didn't think we were on a date," she replied. "But you asked me for a ride," he said. Note that in this case, this Other Rules girl kept her wits about her. She didn't reveal, for example, that this *was* exactly how she would have behaved on a date. She made him wonder.)

If you don't want something like that to happen to you, follow our advice. When you ask your intended (for the evening) to go dancing with you, be very direct. Look him right in the eyes—just like we taught you to—and say, "Would you like to go dancing with me?" We're fairly sure, if you've been dressing like we told you and doing that pouty thing with your lips, he'll die for the opportunity. Otherwise, you can either ask someone else or hijack the first man you see as soon as he has one foot out of the office.

The best thing to do is what we should have been doing in high school: hanging out with the band. Let's face it, rock stars are sexy: They always will be. Even ugly guys make cute rock stars. There are usually two cute guys in any band—one at the very least. Think Joe Perry of Aerosmith. Think Jakob Dylan of the Wallflowers.

Think Keith Richards from the Rolling Stones. (We just slipped him in to see if you were paying attention!)

Wait until the band goes on break and trail after them to the parking lot. Tell them you like the way they sound. Tell them that rock 'n' roll has a long and important history of musician–groupie relations. We'll promise you that they won't ask you any questions. Plus, they'll never make you dance: They're tired of the music, too. They have no desire to groove with you, unless you're talking a very sexy naked samba back at your place.

Of course, dancing on a crowded floor and dancing solo for your lover (or on stage for your lover) are entirely different things. If your goal is to lap-dance your way into your sweetie's heart, by all means go for it. And turn to Rule 15 so that we can give you all the necessary tips!

Rule 7
The Ziploc Liplock—How to Be an Above-Average Kisser

If you haven't at least kissed her mouth, shoulders, neck, breasts, armpits, fingers, palms, toes, soles, navel, genitals, and earlobes, you haven't really kissed her.
—The Joy of Sex

You never know exactly how long you're going to be with a particular man. Men can get boring very quickly. Even the cute ones. This is why you must act quickly when you're with a new man. Very quickly. We recommend that you lock lips with him immediately upon meeting for a date. We're talking somewhere in the first two minutes.

Starting a date with a kiss will serve several functions. First, you won't have to deal with the awkwardness that the beginning of any date can bring. You know, those opening moments after you say "hello" when you're supposed to engage in clever small talk that always seems to revolve around the weather. And while we don't have anything against the weather, who needs to discuss El Niño any more? Second, your breath (and his) is sparklingly minty fresh: You haven't done any drinking or dining yet. Third, kissing right off will allow you to see whether he's got the goods to be a worthwhile lover. (If he fails at this task, you really won't have wasted much time. You can cut the date short with some sort of excuse, put on a fresh coat of lipstick, and head out the door. The bars are probably still open. You can head down to your favorite pub and try out a new set of lips.)

But before you judge him, shouldn't you be sure that *you* know how to kiss? Yes. And, as usual, we're here to help with a handy set of rules about engaging in a kiss, rights and wrongs that you should live by from now on. Actually, there aren't that many wrongs. Don't slobber, of course, but that's about it. Start fast or slowly, depending on how turned-on your date has made you. Kiss with your eyes open or closed, depending on which you like better. If your partner objects to either style, you've got your answer right there: He's *wrong* for you. We like it when men bite our bottom lips, and we advise you to offer yours to be bitten. We do *not* like it when use their tongues as if they were prepping us for a root canal. We think rubbing noses in the style of the "Eskimo kiss" is a little silly (no offense to Eskimos intended), but if you like it, go for it.

The real "how to's" about kissing revolve around *where* you do your kissing. We suggest that immediately after your date rings your bell, as it were, you should open the door, grab him by his necktie, and drag him directly into a mouth-to-mouther. Kiss him passionately. French kiss him, letting your tongues meet and mingle in a delightful little two-step. (Or waltz, if you've got more rhythm than we do.)

Most likely, your date will collapse on your sofa (which you should have positioned him in front of, so as to cushion his fall). He'll look up at you gratefully and start stammering about how happy he is to see you. Surreptitiously, he will reach for the nearest sofa cushion and place it over his groin area. Smile at him while he does this and go and freshen up your lipstick. (We think kissing with lipstick on is ultra-sensuous. You can see the road map of where you've been and you can plan where you're going.)

Once you've let your date catch his breath, we recommend joining him on the sofa, love seat, beanbag chair, or floor, and continuing the experiment. (Of course, if he couldn't keep up with you in the opening round, you should have already ejected him by now.) But assuming you're into his free-form lipstyle, curl up in his lap and give him all you've got. Kiss him on the mouth again and then move down his body, removing his necktie and gently unbuttoning his shirt. Begin an exploration of his chest and stomach. He should be caressing your hair at this point and calling you pretty pet names like "oh" and "kitten" and "baby."

Move back up to his lips and kiss him here some

more. Tease and taunt him. Drive him crazy with lust.
Then tell him to hold on while you read a few more
chapters of this book!

Rule 8

Creamed Corn Wrestling
and Other Activities for a Slow Date

Almost every person has something secret he
likes to eat.

— M. F. K. FISHER

You've been there before, secure-
ly buckled into the passenger
seat of his car, caught in the endless conversation that
goes:

Him: "What do you want to do?"
You: "I don't know…"
Him: "Do you want to see a movie?"
You: "Sure."
Him: "What do you want to see?"
You: "I don't know…"

It's hell, isn't it? You're actually in hell, and you see no way out. Well, baby cakes, that's what we're here for! Before your date, while you're wandering around naked, trying to choose between the Catholic schoolgirl skirt or the zebra-print strapless dress with the matching beaded bag, plan the date.

"But wait," you're saying. "That's what he's supposed to do. He's the guy, right? And guys are supposed to plan everything."

Wrong!

All the guy is truly capable of is showing up. Trust us. We've learned this lesson the hard way. We don't want you to have to learn it all over again. While you're curling your eyelashes and shaving your legs, mentally explore your dating options. If you get stuck, we've listed some below:

CREAMED CORN WRESTLING

This activity is always a hit! All you need is about thirty gallons of creamed corn and a sunken circular bathtub. (Or a big inflatable plastic pool if you want to try this outdoors.) Fill the tub with the creamed corn. Slide into your favorite bikini. Oil yourself up with some butter or margarine. You're set! We assure you that your date will enjoy this activity so much that he may never want to leave your apartment. Be prepared! The next time creamed corn goes on special, stock up!

JELL-O WRESTLING

Sure it sounds a lot like the activity above, but it's not. Jell-O has its own special place in our hearts. It wiggles.

It squooshes. It makes interesting noises when you jump in it. Again, all you need is a large tub, about 1,000 packages of Jell-O, and a willing wrestling partner. If you invite a girlfriend over, too, you can charge money. Men will actually pay to watch you and your girlfriend dive into the gooey stuff! (Diet tip: Use sugar-free Jell-O, and you've got a low-cal snack as well as a fun-filled evening event!) For added variety, you can add marshmallows while the Jell-O is setting, or make a Waldorf salad by adding cream cheese and chopped fruit. Note: Be sure to pick a flavor that your man likes. If he's anti-lime, you don't want to be caught wrestling in the green stuff, so switch to berry or orange, or grape!

PASTA WRESTLING

This one was suggested to us by a friend who swears by it. She thinks that wrapping herself in noodles and sliding around on her beau is one of the most erotic sensations she's ever experienced. We were less sure until she explained that pasta wrestling is done sans spaghetti sauce. She makes enough noodles to feed a football team, throws in a few sticks of butter, and starts slithering around in them. She recommends trying out different shapes of pasta like bow ties, wagon wheels, or shells, although she admits that long, flat egg noodles are her personal favorite. If this appeals to you, or if you're dating an Italian man, by all means go for it. If not, move right on to...

PUDDING WRESTLING

We love this activity! It's really one of our favorite pastimes, even when we're by ourselves. (Although we must admit that doesn't happen to us very often.) Why do we love pudding wrestling so much? Because pudding tastes and feels good. Close your eyes and visualize yourself sinking into a tub filled with vanilla pudding. (Or chocolate. Or butterscotch. Or if you're really adventurous, pistachio.) Now imagine yourself dunking your date in a vat of pudding and then licking him clean. Forget the wrestling! Pudding is the place to be for a ravenous Other Rules girl! (Diet tip: Use skim milk when making the pudding. It feels and tastes just the same when you slide down the side of the tub.)

TAPIOCA WRESTLING

All right, all right, you caught us. Tapioca is actually a type of pudding. But it's got a different texture. A unique texture. A texture that feels very naughty when it's sliding between your toes, fingers, and thighs. There are these tiny little balls of something—we're not precisely sure what—in tapioca. Rolling about in it is like being massaged by millions of tiny little fingers. And now tapioca even comes in cute snack packs you can bring to your office. (Sure, you'd need several million to fill a tub. But if you want to indulge in a bit of nostalgia for a wild night, have tapioca for lunch and let the memories roll!)

WHIPPED CREAM FIGHTS

You can wrestle in whipped cream, too, but we reserve whipped cream for date night fights. Fights are fun. You and your m-o-t-m ("man of the moment") arm yourselves with cans of the stuff and then chase each other around the house, spraying! (It helps if you put plastic slipcovers over the furniture, have linoleum floors, and rent your place instead of own.) We've heard that cheese-in-a-can is also fun for this type of festivity, but we've never really enjoyed the look of yellow squiggles spread over our bodies. White foam is much more appetizing, but try it if you want a change.

For whipped cream wrestling, get out the inflatable pool, go down to your local grocery store, and clean out their Cool Whip section. (Unless you're feeling very Martha Stewart and want to make your own whipped cream from scratch. In which case, you'll need to buy a different book entirely. Because we never have that much time on our hands. Ever.)

Note: While we're all in favor of creativity, we do *not* recommend wrestling in cottage cheese or yogurt (they simply don't stay fresh long enough), or in peanut butter (too sticky), or in oatmeal (too gloopy), or in any type of soup. And, while we haven't ever actually tried it ourselves, we have heard that fondue-wrestling is all the rage in Europe! Turn your hot tub into a fondue pot and dunk yourself right in! You can make a plain cheese or chocolate fondue, or better yet, get a recipe book to help you create a wide range of wild tastes!

Rule 9
Always Answer the Door Naked!

To invite a person into your house is to take
charge of his happiness for as long as he is under
your roof.

—BRILLAT-SAVARIN

So you had a great date. A fabulous date. A mind-blowing,
bed-shaking, neighbors-pounding-on-your-wall date.
He's the man for you. (Or at least the man for this
particular moment. The man until the better man
comes along.) How are you going to keep his interest?
Baby, it's not a problem. Not for an Other Rules girl.

But you already thrilled him to death when he
groped beneath your skirt and hit skin instead of silk.
And you wrestled him in a vat of creamed corn, and
won! How are you going to top that? Repeat these
words: *From now on, always answer the door naked.* He

won't know what hit him. He'll stand gawking on your doorstep, even in the pouring rain, and you'll have to grab him by the tie and yank him into the house before he drowns. Then be gentle. Let him catch his breath and take his coat from him—before you jump his bones.

You say you're not meeting him at home? You're having dinner with his boss, meeting for drinks at a nice restaurant, or going to the opera? (Okay, hold on one second. Can we ask why you're going to the opera? Have you ever had fun at the opera? Has anyone ever had fun at the opera?) Regardless of where you're going, go naked beneath your coat. Any long coat will do. Wear your stockings and garters underneath and nothing else. Choose your sexiest mules. Flash him as soon as you get a moment alone. (Or *nearly* alone. We don't mind if you give the doorman an extra thrill.)

It's cold outside? This isn't a concern, because he's going to be heating you up so quickly that you won't be able to keep the coat on. You'll be lying on top of it, with him on top of you, radiating heat like you wouldn't believe! Strangers will gather around you just to warm their hands.

You've already greeted him naked? Two times? Three times? Every day for a week? And this is the same guy? (Are you *sure*?) Okay, it's time to get out the Saran Wrap. Look, cutie, it's not a cliché if it's new to you. One of our foremothers, Marabel Morgan, knew what she was talking about when she suggested this little doozy! And, in our humble opinion, Saran Wrap is one of the best inventions of this century. In fact, if the Saran Wrap people would let us, we'd love to do an ad campaign for them. (Although it might not be one they could show on daytime television.)

If you're confused or if this is your first time under cellophane, let us help you. Simply wrap your pretty body from under your arms down to your thighs. (Be sure you can still walk to the door or you'll have to call out to him from the kitchen. Which isn't a bad idea, because kitchen sex is some of the hottest sex around.) Did you know that Saran Wrap now comes in a variety of different festive colors, including red, yellow, blue, and green? That's a color for almost every night of the week! Be careful, though: Any Other Rules girl knows that her stilettos should definitely match her wrap!

Once you're all wrapped up as pretty as an X-rated Christmas present, all you'll have to do is wait for your man's reaction. Which we assure you will be positive. Every man we've ever run into has been enamored of an evening devoted to Saran Wrap. Your man will be no different. He'll adore touching you through the slick stuff while still being able to see you. It's an experience that brings out the curious little boy in every man. He'll want to rub up against you. He'll try licking you through it. He'll want to see what happens when it gets wet— and we're sure you'll help him out in this department. Move the party into the shower and experiment as much as you wish. With our blessings!

Bonus: Since you're planning on showering anyway,

you might as well get a little messy. Before he arrives, get out the whipped cream, chocolate sauce, honey, and so on. Line the ingredients up in the kitchen, and invite him to be the chef *chez toi*. He can create a chocolate-covered you, and that's just for starters. He might also dabble in those special Italian syrups used to flavor soda water, coffee, and other drinks. The range is amazing: hazelnut, pineapple, lime, mint, etc. Something to tickle any taste bud!

Rule 10
Ending Your Date With Breakfast

'Tis an ill cook that cannot lick his own fingers.
—SHAKESPEARE

MENU
You

You on toast

You and a soft-boiled egg

For variety, you can try one of these:

Him

Him on toast

Him and a soft-boiled egg (*salt and pepper to taste*).

Any questions?

Rule 11
Picking Up the Tab—
Why You Should (and Must) Pay

I'm tough, ambitious, and I know exactly what I want.

—MADONNA

We know that most of your dates involve few expenses: After all, they happen indoors and under the covers. But some day you might find yourself on a date with a man where you might actually want to do something that costs money. (Although we don't really see why you would. There are so many free public places to play: parks, parking lots, laundromats, the basement of your building, and so on.) But if it turns out that you and your date wind up in a restaurant ordering food (instead of making love on the sink in the ladies' room), at a movie, or playing a round of miniature golf, please follow this rule very carefully: You must pick up the tab.

We know that there are other dispensers of advice out there who will tell you to do the exact opposite. They'll say that if a man doesn't pay he's not all that interested in being with you. Or they'll say that it's more natural for a man to pay because throughout history men have been the providers. But don't listen to these morons! They're just trying to confuse you, princess. They'll tell you that if you pay, he'll think you're pushy, headstrong, or independent. To this we say: Damn straight! You're all those things and more.

If you need more evidence before you whip out your wallet, we'll explain further. Here's why they're wrong: The person who pays has the power. Yes, it's true. You didn't want to hear it, we know. But wouldn't you rather learn it from us than from some crazy person on the street?

You see, when you plunk down your credit card, you might as well be saying, "You're mine for the evening, baby. Better hustle those pretty buns of yours over to the door and hold it open for me!" And if you let *him* pay, or if he somehow manages to slide his charge card to the waiter before you do, then he wins. He owns you, at least for the moment.

Doesn't this explain why so many men reach for their wallets as if it were an automatic response? Their fathers, coaches, or fraternity brothers explained this rule to them long ago. Mentally, each time they're paying they're rubbing their hands together thinking of all the ways you'll have to pay them back! But if you do as we say, then they'll be in your debt instead. Here's how the pay scale works out:

ACTIVITY	COST	REAL COST
You take him out for ice cream	$3	Hot kissing in the car
You buy him a burger and fries	$6	He fondles your breasts
You take him to an arcade	$8	He caresses your butt
You take him miniature golfing	$10	He gives you a hickey
You take him to a movie	$18	Petting in the back row
You buy him dinner	$20	Okay sex
You buy him dinner with wine	$30	Average sex
You buy him steak	$40	Good sex
You take him to a show	$75	Great sex
You take him skiing	$300	Fabulous sex
You take him on a cruise	$1,000	Hours of oral sex
You take him to a hockey game	Doesn't matter	He looks for your G-spot
You take him to a boxing match	Doesn't matter	He finds your G-spot

We recommend cutting out this scale, having it laminated, and keeping it in your pocket book at all times. If he balks, don't you buy it. He knows exactly what the rules are. He was hoping to have *you* in his debt, and now you've beaten him at his own game. If he won't pay up, pull out this chart and show him the exact conversions. Think about it. Wouldn't you rather that he owes you than you owe him? It's up to you, cupcake, but we know where *we* stand!

Rule 12
Call Early, Call Often,
Page Him if Necessary

Women should be obscene and not heard.
— GROUCHO MARX

We like to talk. Have you guessed that yet? We think we have many interesting things to say. Sure, we chat with our girlfriends. Our mothers. Our college roommates. The nice ladies who answer the phones at the Victoria's Secret catalog mail order service. We call them up whenever we have a free moment. But occasionally we like to talk to men, too.

You're probably asking yourself: "Why on earth would you want to talk to men? All men want to discuss is the latest big game. The fastest new car. The tastiest cigar. They never want to talk about lipstick, hair, clothes, perfume, or *any* of the important things!" We'll fix that for you. We'll teach you exactly how to train your man in the art of proper conversation. If that fails, we'll tell you exactly when and how to shut him up. But *first* you have to get him to talk to you.

Some people say that girls shouldn't call guys. They say that it makes a woman appear pushy, needy, or desperate. "Pshaw!" is our response. Forget what those idiots say. They're lonely. And ugly. And frigid. You have a *right* to pick up your phone and call your man whenever you want to. And if you don't have a man, you have a right to pick up your phone and call somebody else's man.

Before you call him, however, we recommend that you work on your sexiest phone voice. Think Marilyn Monroe singing "Happy Birthday" to JFK—(or singing or saying anything else, for that matter). Think Kathleen Turner's ultra-husky tone or Jennifer Tilly's baby-doll lisp. Choose the style you can most easily mimic, and practice whenever possible. Answer your phone at work in this new voice. Order drinks at the bar with your fabulous husky whisper. If you're shy, we recommend that you invite your girlfriends over to help you out. Make a pitcher of margaritas, seat yourselves on the sofa, and talk to each other in your sexy phone voices. If you have any trouble figuring out how to talk sexy, listen to an erotic audiotape or CD, or call up a 976 number and listen to how *those* girls do it!

When you are absolutely ready, call him. Be sure to remind him who you are (the girl who didn't wear panties on the first date, the girl draped in blue Saran Wrap) and what you can do (unroll a condom in the dark with your teeth, contort yourself into a pretzel shape with your feet behind your ears). (Feel free to fill in the blanks with your own favorite skills. We simply used ours.) Wait until he sighs and murmurs your name as he recalls the magical moments you spent together. The way you looked, smelled, and tasted. The way he struggled against the handcuffs in the morning when he tried to get out of bed and get ready for work.

A good phone call will go something like this:

You: "Hi, baby, it's Kiki."

Him: "Kiki…"

You: "I had such a great time the other night."

Him: "Kiki…"

You: "I'm still trying to get the creamed corn out of my carpet."

Him: "*Kiki*…"

You: "But it was worth it."

Him: Sigh…

When he returns from his trip to fantasyland, whisper that you're free for lunch, or dinner, or drinks…. Or if not exactly free, then cheap. And if not exactly cheap, then easy. Most likely, he'll want you to meet him somewhere, and quickly. If he does, you may want to read Rule 18, Love in an Elevator—An Insider's Guide to Outdoor Sex. Brush up on it on the cab ride over. We think it's always best to be prepared!

But what should you do if you try and try, but simply

cannot catch him on the phone? First, let's analyze the situation together.

1. Does he have a secretary who monitors his calls, making him impossible to reach at work? Well, if you're a smart Other Rules girl (and we know you are), you'll befriend her right away. From the very first phone call, you'll be cheerful and funny and ask for her name. Every time you call, you'll say, "Hey, Chelsea, did you know there's a sale at Bloomies?" or "Did you know George Clooney is going to be filming on location nearby?" (Or some other girl-bonding thing.) She'll love talking to you because it means she doesn't have to file for the moment. You're her buddy. You're helping her day go by faster. Pretty soon, she'll put you right through to your man.

2. What if you're calling him at home, and he has an answering machine, and he's one of those obnoxious screeners who might be listening to you blathering on and on while he watches Monday Night Football? Leave him an X-rated message. Go ahead. Tell him exactly what you'd do to his blank with your blank in the back of a blank filled with blank if he were with you. Say it slowly. Huskily. Seductively. If the machine cuts you off, call back and finish the message. Use the most descriptive terminology you can think of. Here's a good message to leave:

"Hi, lover boy, it's Randi. I'm just lying here naked

on my waterbed with a bottle of Wesson oil and my best friend Becki, who's an underwear model. We were thinking of you and wondering whether you were free tonight to come over and play with us. But I guess you're out. [Deep pouty sigh.] So it looks like we'll have to call up someone else...."

If he doesn't *immediately* pick up the phone, it's only because he's shaking so bad that he can't walk without hurting himself. We guarantee he'll call you back. And he'll keep the tape for private listening on his Walkman in bed late at night.

3. What if he has a girlfriend and her voice is on the answering machine, too? Let's say it's a cutesy, bubbly message that makes you feel a little bit sick to your stomach. One of those couple-messages where the two people take turns saying something like:

Him: "We're out right now."

Her: "Or we're *in* right now."

Him: "And we can't come to the phone, can we, cupcake?"

Her: "Giggle!"

Together: "So leave us a message at the beep."

Hang up! Right now! Decide whether this man is worth the effort. (Somehow, his girlfriend was able to talk him into calling her "cupcake" on the outgoing answering machine message, even though he knew his poker buddies would hear him and tease him no end.

Has she got him wrapped around her little finger! Is this really the guy you want?) If so, call him at work instead. If he gave you his number, he doesn't really love Cupcake. He loves *you*. He wants and craves you. She'll be out of the picture in no time at all. We promise.

4. What if he has a wife and it's her voice on the answering machine? No problem. Our motto is that wives are really only serious girlfriends who live in. (Look, we don't mean this in an offensive way. Some of our best friends know people who are married. But all is fair in love and war.) So if you want him, follow the same rules as above. Call him at work, page him, or write him a "nasty" e-mail. He's sure to respond in no time, wedding ring tucked into his breast pocket. Just like before.

For more on dating married men, turn to Rule 24: The Mistress File—How to Date a Married Man.

If you truly can't get through by phone, maybe he's got a job that takes him out in the field, away from civilization, and his cell phone battery just went dead (otherwise he'd have picked up, right?). We suggest paging or e-mail. Paging is fun because you can send him filthy messages that will announce their arrival by vibrating in his pocket. What a good way to make him remember you!

We like e-mail too, but there are some strict rules to remember. If you're both working in the same office, please be sure to write in code. (You don't want prying eyes to easily decipher your messages.) Some geographical acronyms (dating back to the two world wars), include:

BURMA: Be Undressed and Ready, My Angel
NORWICH: k(N)ickers Off and Ready When I Come Home

But those were written for men to send to women. And you need some to send to men, right? Well, choose from these geographical acronyms created for your own personal use!

IDAHO: I Dream About Hot Orgasms
MAINE: My Aching Insides Need Sex
OREGON: Office Romances Enable Great Orgasms Nightly
TEXAS: Tease Each X-rated Anatomy Section
UTAH: Underwear Torn Away, Hooray!

Or create your own. We can't do everything for you, you know!

If you don't work in the same office, you still may want to write coded e-mail. Regardless of how private the electronic world may seem, people are always breaking into other people's computers and reading their mail. (Wives seem particularly adept at this.) We suggest writing titillating mail that can be taken in more than one way. Use as many innuendoes and double entendres as you can possibly work in.

Or simply take a completely different route and write meaningless messages that he can try to decode himself, as in: "Hi Tom. Your laundry's ready. Staci." He knows you never do laundry. So what could you possibly be referring to? His mind will boggle trying to figure out exactly how your message connects with pudding wrestling. We assure you he'll be at your next date early!

Rule 13

Speak, Boy!—Training Your Man in the Art of Conversation

If you haven't got anything nice to say about anybody, come sit next to me.
                    —ALICE ROOSEVELT LONGWORTH

Let's say you got your man on the phone. Or if he wasn't home, then your man did call you back when he received your message. Immediately. Just like a good little man should. But when you spoke to him, the conversation was as dull as dishwater. And we hear that's pretty dull. (We wouldn't know, since—as we said earlier —we don't actually clean anything ourselves. Still, we trust our sources. They've never steered us wrong.)

Just because he's not much of a clever conversationalist doesn't mean you should dump him. He might be very good at other important dating activities. (See the ones listed in Rule 8: Creamed Corn Wrestling and Other Activities for a Slow Date.)

But you're an Other Rules girl, and you'd like your man to talk to you about the important things in life. Which, as all of us Other Rules girls know, do not include sports, any kind of bowl (be it Super, Orange, Sugar, Rose, or Toilet), cars, cigars, stocks, or hunting and gathering. Yet these are the topics that most men seem to want to talk about. So what's an Other Rules girl to do?

Simple, sweetie. Train your man in the art of conversation. Needless to say, you must decide if it's worth it. Is this particular man simply a flavor of the month, week, or afternoon? If you decide this is the case, plug your ears up with a little bit of cotton, smile and nod at whatever he says, and picture that cute black tank dress in the window of Urban Outfitters that you're going to buy this weekend. Or think about those high-heeled sandals with the cork bottoms that Cindy, your friend from work, just bought. Or visualize a Chanel compact. The kind with four different shades of lipstick and those adorable little brushes that come with it.

If you've decided that this man is going to be around long enough that you'll actually have to spend some time talking with him—long enough that he'll figure out you've got cotton in your ears, then you'll need the following items:

- Wires
- Access to an electric outlet
- A loud buzzer

Wait until he begins to blather on about how some team crushed some other team, or about how the Lakers haven't been the same since Kareem, or about how Dennis Rodman did anything. (Wait! If he's talking about Dennis Rodman, there is every chance that clothes, lipstick, sex, or hair colors will come up in the conversation!) Hook him up so that whenever he starts to talk sports, you can give him a mild electric shock, accompanied by a loud noise from the buzzer. If he starts to describe his latest hunting or fishing expedition, buzz him again. This should cure him of his need to describe every single triumph in no time!

If you don't want to get that involved or if you are no good at home wiring, tell him you will be happy to listen if he will perform oral sex on you at the same time. Push him down on his knees, stand above him with your legs spread, and let him keep right on talking. The vibrations from his lips and vocal chords will feel delicious! Let us assure you! Encourage him to talk for hours. Whenever he seems to be slowing down, throw out other sports topics of interest. Yell "Tiger Woods!" or "Dan Marino!" or "Chicago Bulls!"

What if he's made you climax eleven times and his tongue is so tired it can no longer waggle, but he *still* tries to discuss the latest move of the Raiders? Well, dumpling, now's the time to wad up your prettiest silk panties (the ones you keep in your top drawer) and gently put them in his mouth. Be careful not to choke him, of course. But let's face it: Panties in mouth—

problem solved. (Note: This is one time when edible panties are not the way to go! He'll chew his way right through them in no time and go right back to yapping about Mike Tyson.)

What should you do if you're on the phone and he insists on giving you the scores to his morning's tennis match? What if he just won't stop! "6–1, 5–2, 1–6...." There's really no way you can electric-shock him over the phone lines. Or silence him with your spread-apart thighs. So what are you going to do? Well, ladies, here's the deal. In this situation, we recommend *only* calling your man for phone sex. Look, if you wanted to chat, you could talk to your girlfriends, right? They're much more interesting to gossip with than your man.

So when you feel your fingers itching to dial his number, decide whether it's because you have *another* itch you want scratched, or whether you're simply bored with your work day and want to while away the hours discussing the latest scent from Calvin Klein. If it's the former, by all means, call him! Tease him and taunt him. Make him truly desperate to see you by using your sexiest, huskiest whisper. Recreate your last evening together and plan your next one. But if it's the latter, call *us* instead. We love talking about girl stuff. In fact, we just bought this totally amazing black lace body stocking. Is it awesome....

Rule 14
You Left a Message —
Why Didn't He Call You Back?

He's dead.
He's lying in a ditch somewhere.
And his last thoughts were of you.

Rule 15
Tricks of the Trade—
Lap-Dancing Your Way Into His Heart

I never made any money till I took off my pants.
—SALLY RAND

We believe that lap-dancing—good lap-dancing, anyway—begins with stripping. Once you're proficient at dancing on stage while you take off your clothing for an audience of strange, drunken, lonely men who will slide greasy one-dollar bills into your G-string, then dancing one-on-one for any of them won't seem nearly as intimidating. So before we move into the lap-dancing arena, we'd like to cover stripping onstage.

First, you're going to have to quit your day job. Look, cutie pie, no matter how athletic or in shape you are, you're really going to need all your free time to practice your stripping routine. So clean out your desk, cubicle, or cubby. Say good-bye to your coworkers, and head home to your apartment.

Next, wipe any negative thoughts about strippers out of your pretty little head. Stripping, like any type of dancing, is an art form. (Tell yourself this over and over and soon you'll believe it, too.) If you are going to master this craft, you will need to practice. Think of yourself as a ballerina. Ballet dancers put in many hours a day dancing in front of mirrors, holding onto a bar for support as they flex and tone their muscles. You're going to do the same thing. Except your bar will be an upright pole in the center of a stage illuminated by flashing disco lights. And your leotard will be split into two pieces, covered with neon pink sequins, and made of itchy faux leather.

Before trying out for your new job as a stripper, we recommend that you practice for a few weeks at home in front of your bedroom mirror. Choose some raucous music: We like just about anything by the Red Hot Chili Peppers, Sublime, or the Rolling Stones. Next, put on your favorite lingerie—something with lace is always nice—and twirl about in it, kicking up your heels, sinking to hands and knees and crawling, doing everything that strikes you as sexy. Pretend you're a pussycat slinking across the stage. Pretend you're Vivica A. Fox in *Independence Day*. She looked hot strutting her stuff while the aliens took over the planet. All strippers can learn from her!

If you need added incentive, we can suggest several other movies to rent before you get up there and shake your groove thing. Try *Striptease*, *Showgirls* (which is a better movie if you mute the sound), or *Some Like It Hot.* (Boy, did Jack Lemmon know how to shake his maracas!)

Remember this while you practice your sexy mama moves: You're an Other Rules girl. And Other Rules girls are special. We like to tease men. We want them to yearn for us. To beg to get next to us. To reach into their wallets and pull out crisp twenty-dollar bills for us. If you keep these concepts in your mind, your body is sure to relax and follow the steps you tell it to.

We'd like to suggest that you invest in a good wig. (Unless you have naturally long hair.) Using a wig gives you an added accessory. You can toss your hair back and forth. You can lean back and let it sway to the rhythm of the music. You can hide your face in your hair if you get a sudden case of the jitters. And if, horror of horrors, someone you're related to shows up at the club, you have a better chance at not being recognized.

When you feel comfortable—and not *one* second before, sweetie—go to amateur night at a local strip club. (Yes, there's at least one in your town. Just look up "Hip Huggers," or "Bare Elegance," or "Pussycat Lounge" in the Yellow Pages. You'll find it.) Then do your teachers proud and land yourself a job! We know you can do it! We're banking on you!

Once you've gotten into the routine of working nights, it's time to invite your intended to come and watch. In order to heat the object of your desire to his particular boiling point, we recommend that you do a dance onstage before you move to his table to get up close and personal. This way he'll get to see you from a distance, and he'll have time to adjust his pants and squirm a bit before you come over to his table and start getting friendly. From there it's up to you. Climb on top of his table, get between his legs, and take it as far as the management will allow. Some places will let you move to a private room for a little Texas Couch Dancing, a more intimate version of lap-dancing that's sure to get your man all hot and bothered. Others will make you stay out in the main room, but that shouldn't stop you from giving it your all. And remember, whatever you do, you should always be practicing the stares we taught you early on. Do your version of Charo's famous "hoochy coochy" dance. Shake back and forth. Shake 'round and 'round. When his eyes start rolling back into his head, you'll know you're doing it right.

Maybe you don't want to get that involved, though. You have a day job you really like, one that makes more money than stripping (although we can't really think of any on the spur of the moment). If this is the case, you can give always your man a lap-dance in the privacy of your own boudoir. Of course, we think it's fun to make him respect the rules put out by any club. He can look but he can't touch. Beer costs $7.50 a bottle. He must pay you $20 a song. (Make sure there's an ATM nearby.) And those $20s will add up. If you haven't figured it out by now, let us clue you in on the best part about learning how to lap-dance: If the date doesn't go over well, at least you'll have made your rent money.

"I've Never Done That Before"— Reinventing Your Innocence

I am terribly shy, but of course no one believes me. Come to think of it, neither would I.

—CAROL CHANNING

Let's say, just for fun, that you like a guy. Really like him. Like him more than the other guys you've been out with. All of the many other guys you've been out with. And now that you've started thinking about it, you don't really want your new fellow to know exactly how many other guys you've been out with. (Even though there's nothing wrong with it. Not a thing! We know women who have dated twice the guys you have! Really.)

Let's just say you want to preserve your reputation. Or invent a whole new reputation. Because maybe he's started into you with the "You tell me about your past and I'll tell you about my past" type of thing. He's being cute and flirtatious, making puppy-dog eyes at you and telling you that he loves you no matter what you've said or done. He's even saying that he thinks it's sexy that you've been with other people. That he finds it a turn-on and wants you to describe the best sex you've ever had in your life. And you're starting to waver, because he sounds sincere. All the same you're worried that later he's going to use the information against you during some huge fight. You're right. He will, believe us.

Let's say you want to wipe the slate clean. Or at least make it a little bit cloudier. Well, we see nothing wrong with that. People find (or rediscover) religion late in life. Why can't you rediscover your innocence? Ready? Then follow the quick and easy steps below:

How to Be a Born-Again Virgin

First, forget everything you've ever done sexually. Picture that button on your computer that says "erase hard drive" and conjure the equivalent for your romantic life. Forget that you know how to undo a man's jeans with your teeth. Forget that you spent hours learning how to unroll a condom with your lips. Forget that you found that special trigger spot on a man called his "perineum" and you know that if you tongue it lightly he will sign over the deed to his house. Forget it all. When you're with *this* man, you're as fresh as a daisy. Keep repeating to yourself, "I've Never Done That Before," and you'll get the idea.

When you go out with this guy, act coy and shy. Lower your lashes. Blush (if you still can). If you can't remember how, then stand in front of the mirror and relive all of the most embarrassing things that have ever happened to you. Focus on each and every one. The time your skirt got tucked into your underwear and you walked down the hall without knowing it. The time you forgot to tell your boyfriend you had used Vagisil, and he went down on you, and his tongue and lips got numb. You were too embarrassed to tell him, so you blamed it on the new bubble bath you'd used, but then you told your roommates because you thought it was funny. And they told all their friends. And people started calling you "Vagi-girl." Or how about that time you walked into the guys' bathroom instead of the girls'? Oh, wait. That turned out okay for you, didn't it?

If he tries to touch you, squirm slightly. Think young. Think innocent. Think about anything except sex. Disregard the fact that your body is saying, "Yes, yes, yessss!" Override your normal, animal instincts and make your mouth say, "No, no, no! I couldn't, really!"

Basically we're telling you that you should be playing hard to get. On the first date, refuse to let your date get past first base. On the second date, let him get to second. And so on. Each step of the way, feign ignorance. Let him help you. Fake it for the sake of your reborn virginity.

Let us point out that even if you don't want to be a born-again virgin, you can have a lot of fun playing the part with your man! Get into a white baby-doll dress with ruffles. Tie pink ribbons in your hair. Ask him to teach you how to do things. He'll love it. He'll get to show you the ropes. The handcuffs. The heated body oil. He'll get to seduce his first love all over again.

RULE 16A:

A codicil to this rule is "Duh, the Subtle Art of Playing Dumb." If you have trouble masking your intelligence, just tell yourself the following: I should never make eye contact with my man. I should never stare. I should never make the first move. Repeat these rules until your mind goes blank. Then you're ready to play dumb and let him have the fun of being the aggressor.

At least, for just one date.

Rule 17
"You Are Soooo Big" —
Learning How to Lie

Illusion is the first of all pleasures.   —VOLTAIRE

This lesson comes right on the heels of reinventing your innocence. And it should. When you were innocent, you used to be more interested in pleasing men, right? But now the older, wiser, and jaded you is usually more involved in pleasing yourself. And that's just fine. But we have found—through extensive interviews of our closest and dearest friends and lovers—that men respond better to women who fudge the truth.

We have to be clear here. We don't condone lying about anything that would damage a lover. You must come clean about your sexual history if it involves his safety. But as far as lying to stroke his ego, well sugarplum, the sky is the limit.

Men are insecure creatures. They're worried. They're concerned. They wake up in the middle of the night screaming: "I'm too small for her! I know it! I'm too small!"

Ultimately, they want to please you. They want to make the earth shake for you. And they want to know that they have the absolute biggest sword of any pirate you've ever been with. Let them think this. Let them tell their friends that they take you places you've never been. (At least, not without the help of a vibrator.)

Lying is easy. Just open your eyes really wide and make direct eye contact with your man. Talk in a slightly baby-doll voice and say, "Oh yes, you are the biggest man I've ever been with. Really." If you want to elaborate, say: "At first I couldn't believe it, but now I see that I am very, very lucky."

Of course someday a man really will be the biggest and you won't have to lie. At some point in your sexual experimentation, you will sleep with the biggest man you've ever slept with. (We recommend you hold onto him.) But if, by some unlucky chance, he slips away from you, then every other man you're with after him will not be the biggest.

But they don't have to know that.

Men are easy to lie to. They will believe it if you say it. So whisper it in his ear, coo it to him while you make love, rent out the billboard near his house and spell it out in six-foot letters. He needs to believe this in order to relax and please you. It's a small price to pay to boost him up and in the long run, a pretty humane thing to do. So do it. Yes, now.

Then prepare to reap the benefits!

Rule 18
Love in an Elevator—An Insider's Guide to Outdoor Sex

It doesn't matter what you do in the bedroom as long as you don't do it in the street and frighten the horses.

—MRS. PATRICK CAMPBELL

You've thrilled him with Saran Wrap (in all of the available colors). You've lap-danced your way right into his heart (and quite possibly his will). You've wrestled him in a vat of creamed corn. And won. What are you going to do now, Other Rules girl?

You're going to Disneyland!

But why? Disneyland is for kids, right? What could you possibly do at Disneyland?

Have public sex, of course!

Yes, it's time to bring out the exhibitionist inside you. Let her roam free. Listen to what she has to say. If the exhibitionist in you is out right now, showing off her red lace bra to strangers on the street, don't worry. We're here to help. But first, it's up to you to decide exactly how far you're willing to go. You may need to refer to our occupation/level of exhibitionism chart (see below):

OCCUPATION	LEVEL OF EXHIBITIONISM
Co-ed	These are the best years of your life. Don't let them go to waste! Make love on the roof of every frat house on campus! Then do it again!
Lawyer	Put yourself on display at every opportunity. You'll always be able to convince people that it wasn't you. *You're* completely innocent!
Senator	Exhibit yourself only at home! (You don't want your story in the tabloids, do you?)
Movie star	Check your ratings. Are you at the top? Then keep your sex habits under wraps.
Fading star	Are you slipping? Do it in the limo on the way to the next gala event. (You want your story to appear in the tabloids, don't you?)

Dental hygienist	Reach for the stars, baby! For some reason men always find dental hygienists very sexy! The more public sex you have, the better.
Beautician	You've got a very sexy job. One that allows you the opportunity to thrill your clients with news of your most recent exploit. So exploit away!
Teacher	Do not get caught in public. Ever! But do consider smuggling your man in to have sex on your desk. What a fantasy come true for any man who had a crush on his teacher!
Editor of an erotic magazine	The sky is the limit. People already think you're a slut. Why not live up to their expectations?
Author	You have total freedom. *Nobody* knows what authors look like! Do it wherever you want! In the backs of bookmobiles. In dark corners of libraries. At book signings. If someone minds, lie and say you're Anaïs Nin. By the time they realize she's dead, you'll be long gone.

Did we leave you off our list? Don't frown, baby doll. This simply means you'll have to judge for yourself. If you don't mind people seeing your panties, or lack thereof, you can have a blast. And why *should* you mind? We only go through life once. Might as well make it fun—and in our world, fun means sex outdoors! On the beach, in an elevator, on an escalator, in a public park, in a cemetery, in your neighbor's backyard, on a cable car, in a movie theater, and so on. Choosing places is easy. What you really need to do is prepare. To that end, here's another handy list of suggested places to play based on your occupation:

OCCUPATION	LOCATION
Artist	Studio
Florist	Greenhouse
Operator	Phone booth
Truck driver	Front seat
Waitress	Kitchen, counter, back booth
Nurse	Doctor's examining room
Dental hygienist	Patient's chair, preferably with the patient
Hairstylist	Swivel chair
Taxi driver	Back of the cab
Lifeguard	Poolside
Aerobics instructor	In the locker room
Musician	In the orchestra pit
Architect	On a drafting table
Actress	On stage (What, you, shy?)

Of course, there *are* other places to play in public. And even if you fit under one of the above categories, it doesn't mean you can't have public sex somewhere else, too. We like rooftop sex, backyard sex, and hot tub sex—just to name a few. So if you have your mind set on exploring the great outdoors, follow the simple tips listed below:

• Find a willing man. (Follow the first few chapters of this book in order to snag a live one—reread them if necessary.)

• Make a date. This doesn't call for a lot of planning in advance. Simply call him, state the place and time, and the planned activity. He'll be there. We promise.

• Wear easy-access, tearaway clothing like the following: A dress or skirt. No pants. (What are you, nuts?) No panties. (Life will be much easier if you follow this rule!) Garters or thigh-highs. No pantyhose.

• Meet him at the designated spot: elevator, escalator, park bench, back row of the movie theater.

• Do what it is the two of you do so well together. (We don't need to spell it out, do we? You've been paying attention, haven't you?)

• Be ready to run if you're caught. Or, be ready to lie! (Need help in this arena? Reread Rule 17.)

Rule 19
Love in a Moving Vehicle

Curve: The loveliest distance between two points.
—MAE WEST

Planes, trains, automobiles, submarines, surfboards, seesaws, cable cars, camels, cement mixers, Harleys, hovercrafts, hot-air balloons, buses, boats, boogie boards, roller coasters, rocket ships, and recreational vehicles: We love making love in or on them all. But just because you've joined the Mile High Club—twice—doesn't mean you've experienced all there is to experience in a moving vehicle. We'd like every Other Rules girl to have made it in a taxi, on a metrorail, on a train, in the back of a limo, in an aerial ride at an amusement park, and so on.

Make a list of the places you'd like to see through half-closed eyes. Then find a willing partner to help you carry out your plan. (For an Other Rules girl, this really shouldn't be difficult.)

Here are a few tips:

• If on a boat with your beloved, be sure that neither one of you gets seasick. There is nothing less romantic than a partner who is green around the gills!

• If making love on an airplane, choose an off-time if you do it in the bathroom. If you and your honey go right after a movie, you'll hold up a huge line and people will start to pound on the door. This may excite you, or it may not, but we've found it a tad annoying. Try the middle of the night, or during the flick, or while the flight attendants are wheeling their carts down the aisle (no one can get through to bother you). If all else fails, knock on the door of the cockpit. The pilots are probably bored. They've done this flight a zillion times. They might let you and your lover in if you promise to put on a good show!

• If in a car, we're guessing that he's doing the driving while you're doing him. And all we can say is that, by God, he'd better be grateful! He'd better make it up to you at the next rest stop! And he'd better choose a straight road!

• If on a submarine, watch out. We're guessing that you smuggled yourself on board. And once the rest of the crew finds out that you're a woman, well, they'll just have to line up and take a number, right?

• If you're on a rocket ship to the moon, hey, girl, we applaud you. Wow! Sex in a gravity-free environment. Now that's cool.

Rule 20
What to Give Him
for Birthdays or Holidays

Even if you only have two seconds, drop everything and give him a blow job. That way he won't really want sex with anyone else.   —JERRY HALL

Say it's his birthday or Valentine's Day or Halloween or Boxing Day or Columbus Day or President's Day (you get the picture), and you want to get him something really nice. Something special. Something he'll never forget. We approve! Absolutely! Go right ahead, with our blessings.

Some people say that men are the ones who should be doing the gifting. That if he doesn't provide you with something worthy of your loveliness, like jewelry or roses or candy, you should dump him. We laugh at this. Come on, now. Guys hate shopping. Why should he have to do something that you actually enjoy? We suggest that you buy yourself something nice whenever the occasion presents itself, and give your man a bonus because that's the kind of Other Rules girl you are!

We've known a lot of guys (we're not bragging here, it's true). And in writing this book, we contacted many of them to ask them specific questions. (Research, can we say, has never been more fun!) For this particular question, we asked guys to tell us about their favorite gifts.

The most-requested presents for guys, excerpted from our poll, are:

• "What I really enjoy is when a woman gives me a blow job. I mean, it's a gift she makes herself. I can't think of anything I'd like to get more."—Mick J.

• "I have to admit that I like a girl who knows how to eat a peter. That's the best quality a date can have, as far as I'm concerned!"—Peter F.

• "As a mechanic, I like a girl who knows her way around an engine. I think the best present a girl could give me is her lipstick on my dipstick."—Dieter M.

• "The best present I ever received was from a girl who played in the same orchestra I did. I'm a horn player. She was a piccolo player. And boy could she get her lips around my instrument!"—Aaron R.

• "I sell vacuums for a living, door-to-door. I've had plenty of experience cleaning the floors of strangers. My favorite gift, however, was when a girl hoovered me instead!"—Max L.

• "My favorite present is when my date gives me a hum job. She can hum any tune she likes, as long as her lips are around my harmonica."—Bob D.

• "One Christmas my girlfriend gave me a gift from France. She had learned how to *faire une pipe* the Continental way and boy was it great! —Sam G.

• "The best date I ever had was one with an athletic girl. Her favorite sport? Tonsil hockey. She played it all night long on my birthday!"—Ralph Q.

• "I was dating this girl from Alabama. What a sweet thing she was. Whenever I showed up at her place she greeted me with a dose of good old-fashioned charm and a proper down-South mouth-hug. I'll tell you, I never was late for a date!"

• "A girl I was seeing gave the best blow jobs I'd ever experienced. On Valentine's Day, she decided to top even herself. She and her best friend took turns going downtown on me. They were both dressed like Playboy bunnies, complete with the little furry tails."—Hugh H.

So there you have it. All of these gifts are, as Mick J. indicates, ones a girl should make herself. But not without a little practice. To be exceptionally good at giving a blow job, you must really enjoy it. Judge to see how your man is responding. Start slowly and get more intense as his arousal grows. And remember this quote from Anatole France: "I prefer the errors of enthusiasm to the indifference of wisdom." Do your best and have fun: Your guy will let you know what he likes the most.

Of course, if you don't think any of those ideas are special enough, we have another suggestion:

Turn yourself into a human éclair. Encase yourself in flaky pastry and slather one side with chocolate frosting from head to toe. Have yourself delivered to his office. He'll think you're wild. And so will his boss.

Rule 21
Dressing for Sex

My husband is German; every night I get dressed up like Poland and he invades me.

—BETTE MIDLER

You've thought about it, haven't you? Fantasized about making love to a cop, firefighter, or sailor. And so has he! Well, maybe not exactly those particular occupations. His fantasies probably range more toward the Playboy bunny, cocktail waitress, or supermodel. But we're really talking about the same thing: turning fantasies into realities. And one easy way to do this is to introduce role-playing into your relationship. More simply put, start playing dress-up.

Say you're interested in bedding a construction worker, but as chance would have it, your current boyfriend is an accountant. Well, cutie, all you need is a tool belt and hard hat and you can turn Mr. Number

Cruncher into one of those guys who sits on street corners and cat-calls you and your girlfriends when you walk by. (Actually, we have to admit that you'll probably have more fun with the real thing. Dump your accountant, slide into your tube top and tight jeans, and head down to that construction site. You'll be glad you did!)

But what about dressing for your man? What about making *his* dreams come true? There was a time—we won't tell you how long ago, it makes us feel old, *sigh*—when we would have said you shouldn't wear anything to have sex. Ever. We would have told you that naked is *always* the hippest (and the cheapest!) way to go. And we even would have reminded you that your man should consider himself extremely lucky just to get close to the bare-bodied you! He shouldn't need extra frills to start his engine.

But what did we know? We were young. We were foolish. We hadn't been paying attention in science class when the teacher explained the concept of gravity, and just what it can do to the female form. And so we are amending our positions. (Not that we were *wrong* before. We're never really wrong. It's just that now we're *more* right.) As modern Other Rules girls, we think it's fun to get gussied up for a night of romping. (Or, if not gussied, then slightly trussed, with underwire push-up bras, corsets, girdles and so on.) So, while naked is still fine and dandy, do not hesitate to doll yourself up when—and if—you want to.

First, look through your ABCs of sexy dressing and

choose the appropriate attire for your particular erotic expedition. Personally, we prefer to plan in themes. If this idea works for you, follow right along. We're here to help you put together six sexy outfits to spring on your current boy toy.

CATHOLIC SCHOOL GIRL

You can be a "good girl" (the quotes *are* intentional) in white cotton panties, a plaid pleated schoolgirl skirt, and a simple twin set. Although dressed like the sweetest young thing on the planet, you'll really be acting like a bad girl in good-girl clothing, which can be extremely exciting. For you *and* him. And if by chance your man-of-the-moment went to Catholic school, he will be unable to believe his luck (and probably unable to contain himself). You will be a fantasy of his from long ago *finally* coming to fruition. But if Catholic school girl just isn't your thing, have no fear! Move right on to...

BETTIE PAGE

With a little creativity in the leather apparel department (and a little help from a brunette wig if you're a blonde), you can quickly transform yourself into another Bettie Page. This famous vixen was photographed many times in totally risqué outfits. For the rest of her look, you'll need high heels and a black bra, panties, and stockings. For the more adventurous, add some kind of spanking implement and a naughty female friend. But if that stretches your limits, as your shrink would say, try...

JANE OF THE JUNGLE

For a completely different look, you can play-act as Jane, Queen of the Jungle. All you need is an adorable primate for a sidekick, a skirt made of palm fronds, and a coconut shell bra. (Oh, wait! Maybe that's the outfit for a Hula girl fantasy. We forget. But either way, it works!) For added arousal, drape your boudoir with real vines and hang bunches of bananas from the posts of your bed. Their aroma is sure to arouse the great ape in any man. But if this look is more involved than you want to get, try...

'40s FILM STAR

If you've been feeling "glamour deprived" lately, play at being a '40s screen star. Think Ava Gardner. Claudette Colbert. Myrna Loy. Exploit your femininity to the max by draping your supple body in a silk robe with a feather collar, low-cut satin nightie, and high-heeled marabou-topped bedroom slippers. Pearls and a martini are two nice additional touches. (We must add that it helps if you have a swashbuckling leading man. If you dress up frilly and your man is a low-brow lunk, you'll be wasting your time. There. We said it. Somebody had to.)

If you feel silly dolled up in your prettiest finery, why not get a little edgier instead, with...

NURSE NANCY

We recommend buying an outfit from one of those sexy catalogs that somehow finds its way into your mailbox every once in a while. You don't want a real nurse's uniform (too dumpy); you want something tight and white with low cleavage. Make this a more exciting experience for both of you by stocking up on Vaseline and rubber gloves. Isn't it time for his annual check-up? But if you're not into this scenario, why not go all the way back in time to the first really sexy woman…

EVE

For this outfit all you need are fig leaves, an apple, and a snake. We recommend punching holes in the leaves and threading them together with yarn. Tie some of them around your waist for a skirt; fashion the others into a cute little bra. (You must be fairly secure with your body before you try out this role-playing situation. But as women who have experienced the fun of being evicted from Eden, we must say that if you can pull it off, this one's worth the effort!)

The positive aspects of each of these outfits is that they're versatile: You can socialize in them, wear them to your favorite bar, go to a concert, to work, anywhere, and then return home with your man to an evening of homemade fireworks. If you don't believe us, just open any fashion magazine and see what the editors are suggesting you wear. Did you catch the recent fad of cashmere sweaters paired with bikini bottoms and chain belts? Now, there's a look that Other Rules girls can really sink their teeth into.

We should point out that you're not the only one

who should be dressing for sex. Your beau needs to know that he can improve himself, too. If he's shy, well by all means, cutie, you can do the dressing for him. Snag him some silk heart-patterned boxers (remember Bruce Willis in *Moonlighting*?). Buy him a pair of tight vinyl hot pants or one of those adorable little leopard-print thongs. This last one should bring out the Tarzan in your boy. If he's receptive, you might even get to have jungle sex: steamy, humid, vine-entangled. Whew! *We're* getting hot just thinking about it.

Rule 22
Tom, Dick, or Harry—
Dating Two (or More) Men at Once

Too much of a good thing can be wonderful.
—MAE WEST

You're a complicated girl. You've got a million passions, an infinite amount of likes and dislikes. It can be difficult—or impossible—to find one guy who can fill all your needs. Plus, sometimes we girls have a hard time making choices. Who wouldn't have a hard time making choices when the world is 50% men, and so many have cute behinds? Moreover, there are lots of benefits to multiple dating. If one of your men decides to call it quits, no worries. You still have a date for Saturday night...and Sunday night...and Monday night. Your dance card is always full!

What's a girl to do if she's got more than one man on

121

her speed dial? Well, for an Other Rules girl, it's as easy as one, two, three (or more). Simply follow our time-tested rules to worry-free multiple dating.

We'll start with the basics. Forget about being on a first-name basis with guys. This will only confuse you, and it may give you away. At least one of them will catch on if you call him by another man's name. (Especially in moments of heated passion.) So when the phone rings and you can't immediately place the voice, simply coo: "Hello, darling." Or when you're in bed, doing what it is you do in bed, and his name escapes you, sigh: "Yes, baby, yesss…"

If you're clever, you can get onto an endearments-only level after just one date. (And we know you're clever, because you're an Other Rules girl!) Of course, the other way to solve this problem is to date only men who have the same first name. We are friendly with a woman who has exclusively dated "Daves" all her life. If you want to try this trick, pick a name you like—obviously, a popular one like Sam, Mike, or Steve works much better than an obscure moniker like Xavier—and go for it! Try to meet men at places where name tags are worn or where place cards are visible, like conventions or bar mitzvahs.

Assuming you've got a few men already adding sparkle to your life, we have one important bit of advice: *stay focused*. Not on the men, silly, but on your apartment. Don't leave any signs around your place that indicate you are not a one-man woman. We advise unplugging your phone (or at the very least, turning off your ringer) when one of your men is over for a visit. You don't want to be in the midst of something sticky when the phone rings and another man (whose name most likely won't spring to your lips) rings up, forcing you to call *him* "baby" while another "baby" glares at you with angry eyes.

Staying focused on your apartment also means: Hide any stray boxer shorts, lose the ticket stubs to the big fight, keep the handcuffs under the bed, and store the condom box in a locked drawer. (If a man notices the condoms are disappearing faster than he's putting them on, the jig is up.)

What if you are currently dating just one fellow and want more excitement? Follow our lead and think like a guy. Oh, we hate to say it. Really, we do. But guys are known for their ruthlessness when it comes to dating. They're always ready to play hard ball, and their pockets are always filled with phone numbers.

So what's an Other Rules girl to do? Act like a guy. If you see someone you want but you're in a relationship, get a number anyway. (Be sure that you get his number rather than giving him yours. You don't want him to call you at an inconvenient time!) Remember, you don't have to act on the situation immediately. But we find that it's especially ego-boosting to have an abundance of phone numbers when you and your significant other are having a fight. It reminds you that men—many men—are out there. And they're waiting for you.

And that's the whole point of being an Other Rules girl, isn't it? A busy—sometimes *very* busy—and happy social life.

Rule 23
What to Do if You'd Rather Date His Roommate

My favorite thing is to go where I've never been.
—DIANE ARBUS

After five nights at your pad, your new beau has finally taken you back to his place for a night of fun and frolicking. The two of you are going it at it on his waterbed when you suddenly hear the distinct sounds of lovemaking—someone else's lovemaking—occurring very close by. Your man is still somewhere in la-la land, biting the back of your neck, licking the point of your stiletto heel, moaning how good your edible panties taste—but you're frozen, listening to what sounds like a better party than yours!

You close your eyes and try your best to get back into the swing of things. You are, after all, an Other Rules girl, and you would never be rude and break his concentration. You simply file away the information to return to later…say, as you stumble down the hallway on your way to the bathroom. And now through the partially open bedroom door across the hall you see *the roommate.* His muscled arms are entwined around a pretty redhead. The trapeze above the bed is still gently swinging back and forth. Shredded sheets cover the carpet and feathers slowly flutter down to Earth. Did they have a good time or what? And now you're realizing that your good time—which was, of course, complete with ingestible massage oils, paraffin candle wax, and a pair of elbow-length black silk gloves— somehow pales in comparison.

While you stand in the bathroom brushing your teeth with your finger, you find yourself wondering what would happen if, instead of kissing your new m-o-t-m goodnight, you slid into his roommate's bed and joined that fiesta?

Well, let us say this: *Don't do it.* Shhhh, don't get worked up. Yes, you can definitely can have the roommate. We're not ogres. We're going to get you everything your sinful little heart desires. But don't make a play for him yet. For now, be an observer: On your way back to your m-o-t-m's bedroom, stand in the roommate's doorway for a moment and survey the surroundings. Then return to neutral ground—your apartment—to do some serious soul-searching.

You have a difficult decision to make. You need to figure out whether you want to ditch your current lover entirely or whether you'd like to simply *add* his room-mate to the fray. Think about it: two men, one apart-ment, and you. If you find this appealing, you've got an extremely easy job ahead of you. Follow this simple procedure. Do you remember the game "Quarters" from college? Now's the time to practice it with your girl-friends until you get very, very good at it.

Once you've thoroughly mastered the game, go to the nearest convenience store and buy several six-packs of beer and one bottle of tequila. Bring the liquor with you on your next date with your guy. Have your guy ask his roommate to join you in some sort of nameless cele-bration. Say you'll explain everything when you arrive.

As soon as you're happily ensconced on the green shag-carpeted floor of their living room, pull out a quarter and challenge the boys to a drinking game. They're going to be macho and try and get you drunk. Which is fine, since you've been practicing for weeks and will be able to hold your own!

When everyone is good and happy, change the game to "Truth or Dare." When it's your turn, dare them to get dirty with you. (Not *physically* dirty, unless you're interested in that sort of thing.) Say that you've always had a fantasy about making it with two hunky lovers, but you've never had the chance to turn this fantasy into a reality. Use the various stares we taught you way back when. The Eyelash Flutter will work particularly well if you throw it in as you make your confession.

The boys will probably look at each other for a long

moment. It's a big commitment they're about to make. They're going to see more of each other than they ever dreamed of or wanted to. But if you're dolled up in your normal Other Rules attire, and if you've been doing your stare right and pouting your lips correctly, then get ready to be swinging on that trapeze, baby. You're about to experience a little bit of heaven.

What if you want to get rid of the first roommate while moving on to the second? You've got a choice. Do you want to pit two boys against each other, make them battle it out for your affections, and perhaps destroy their friendship entirely? Or do you want to move in quietly and begin an illicit affair with roommate number two, leaving roommate number one high and dry? If this is the case, we have five words of advice for you: Invite him to *your* place. You can have the most mind-blowing sex in the world with the roommate, and your boyfriend (now ex-boyfriend, we're guessing) will never be the wiser. We want you to have everything life has to offer, princess. But in this case, you can do it without hurting (really hurting) the man you used to love, or at least like (sort of).

If you choose to let the boys battle for your attention, let us prepare you for one horrible possibility: Your ex and his roommate may team up against you. If they decide that, although quite desirable, you're not worth losing their friendship over, they may hatch their own devilish plan to make you pay. Which is why we recommend dating undercover. Plus, illicit sex is the best sex. We've said it before, and we'll say it again.

Oh, one last possibility. What if your boyfriend's roommate is a girl, and it's *her* affections you're after? Well, sugar dumpling, we'll give you plenty of advice in this department later on. For now, let's just say that if you want to keep your current man, you must initiate an important conversation with him. Pay attention: It's best to do this while you're having sex. Confess that you've always been curious about what it would be like to be with a woman, but you've never found a guy who could understand. Say that what you really need is a man who could be there for you to help you through it. Literally. Your guy will probably have a heart attack on the spot. *Let it be me*, he'll say to you, and *This is soooo cool*, he'll say to himself. Soon he'll be saying something along those lines to his friends, the guys at the gym, and strangers in the grocery store. Men *love* the thought of two girls kissing...and more. Simply describe what you wish you could do with his roommate, and add him to the scene, too. Watching, joining in, whatever he'd like. Then proceed with the Quarters plan outlined above, and let the bras fall where they may!

Rule 24
The Mistress File—
How to Date a Married Man

The world wants to be cheated. So cheat.
—XAVIERA HOLLANDER (A.K.A. THE HAPPY HOOKER)

Lots of people will tell you not to date a married man. And we agree. Absolutely! Don't date a married man. Date at least two, preferably three. If you're going to cross that barrier, you might as well go for the gold. After conducting extensive research (in a small town on the border of Sweden) we have found that the guilt you'll experience for dating one married man is equal to the guilt for dating three or more. And if you're dating three, let's face it: You'll get three times the gifts, three times the expensive restaurants, and three times the sex.

The actual dating of a married man (or men) is simple. In fact, it's probably going to be one of the easiest things you've ever done. The only difficult part of dating a married man is (in our humble opinion) dealing with your conscience. But if you're reading this chapter, and if the concept of an extramarital affair didn't make you throw the book across the store and go off storming in search of the manager, you probably don't have a conscience. So don't worry.

When you date a married man, you have to do very little. He's so grateful that you're going out with him, having sex with him, and treating him the way women used to treat him before he got married, he's going to be forever in your debt. He'll buy you flowers, jewelry, clothes. He'll take you anywhere you want to go and then some. He'll follow you around like a puppy dog.

But first, you're going to have to meet a married man. This step is cake. Open your eyes. Married men are walking right outside your window! There's one! And there's one! And look over there!

The greatest thing about married men is that someone else has already given them the seal of approval. But don't be lulled into complacency. Just because a man has a ring doesn't mean he's a good date. How can you weed the losers from the winners? This is easier than it sounds. (Like we said, all parts of this rule are simple.)

• Watch him. Does he get teary-eyed when one of those "a diamond should represent two months' salary" commercials plays on the TV over the bar? Turn your back and walk away.

• Listen to him. Does he talk about his wife a lot? In glowing terms? Cross him off your list.

• Look at him. Does his wife dress him? (It should be obvious.) If so, don't think about dating him. He doesn't have any spine. You want someone with his own sense of style, not to mention the ability to tie his own tie.

Being the other woman has a lot of advantages. It means never having to pack his lunch or take his shirts to the cleaners. It means only having to look your best on the few nights he can sneak away to visit you. The rest of the time you are free to see other men or, if you feel like it, stay home in your favorite pjs and talk on the phone to your girlfriends. Most importantly to an Other Rules girl, being an other woman means you'll probably be having really good sex. Married men have had lots of sexual experience. And you'll be having illicit, you're-going-to-go-to-hell-for-it sex with them. It's the best stuff on earth, let us tell you.

When involved with a married man, be sure to remember one important thing: Do not fall in love with him. (Write this down on your "to don't" list.) Falling in love with a married man is taboo for a mistress! It's the biggest mistake you can make. If you date a married man without falling in love, you can be relaxed and carefree. You can enjoy your time with him and your time apart. But if you fall for him, your world will turn upside-down. You'll be jealous of every moment he spends with her instead of you. You'll start calling his house at all hours and driving around and around his block to see if you can catch just one glimpse of him. What a horrible, non–Other Rules girl type of existence!

But, princess, what if you foolishly ignore our advice? You've fallen in love with him, you want to wear his ring. Please be sure this is honestly what you want. Think about how he complained about his wife to you. Now you'll be assuming her role. Is it the role you want? It is? Well...

If you've weighed the facts and decided you do need him, then go ahead and follow the tips listed in Rule 25: Staking Your Claim—Getting Rid of the Competition, Permanently. But first, we do need to inform you about something we call "Mistress Karma." If he leaves her for you, there is a 99.9% chance that he will leave you for someone else. Someone younger and prettier than you. It will shatter your self-esteem and you'll come crying to us, but we'll just shake our heads at you. So if you think the few moments with him as yours and yours alone are worth it, fine.

But don't say we didn't warn you.

Rule 25
Staking Your Claim—Getting Rid of the Competition, Permanently

Never let go of what you're holding until you've got hold of something else.
— THE FIRST LAW OF WING-WALKING

Let's say, just for the fun of it, that you're getting used to your man-of-the-moment. You think he's pretty cute, pretty special, and pretty darn clever with a certain part of his anatomy. But let's also say, again for the fun of it, that you get the feeling you may not be the only special someone in your lover's life. (Or perhaps you're dating a married man—in which case you know you're not the only one—and you've decided that instead of being the other woman, you want to be the only woman.)

What's an Other Rules girl to do when she wants a man all to herself?

Stake your claim! We don't want you to think that

just because you are practicing the Other Rules you shouldn't have a boyfriend. We said early on that you should have boyfriends by the dozen. But if it turns out that you want a specific one—if a different one every night isn't working for you—then, honey, hold onto the one you have. And hold onto him with your lips....

We're talking monkey bites, hickeys, love bites. Whatever you call them, they're very sexy. Every time he sees these little reminders, he'll think of you and your sweet little mouth. And the angelic way you grab hold of his skin and suck, suck, suck! And not only will he be thinking of you, so will whomever he goes out with next. This is why it's important to make your hick-eys count. Or, better still, count your hickeys! On the first night, give him one in an obvious place like his neck. He'll either show it off proudly at work or to his buddies over beers at the corner pub. Or he'll develop a sudden desire to be British, and he'll walk around with an ascot.

On the second date, when you decide you really like him, give him two. One on the neck, and one somewhere lower on his anatomy—say, his belly. This way, if another woman gets past the ascot, she'll see that someone has already been to the region she's exploring. And she will either demand to know who else he's been seeing or, if she's an Other Rules girl, will up the ante herself.

On the third date, give him three, and so on. Of course, you know that most men will want to return this particular favor. If you're doing a multiple dating thing yourself, be prepared to give your other beaux an explanation for those juicy marks appearing on your neck (or elsewhere). And when you come up with a plausible explanation, could you please send it to us? We've never thought of one ourselves.

If you just don't want to get that involved, you can stake your claim in a variety of ways. Spray his clothing with your perfume before he leaves your apartment. Think like a skunk when you do this. We're not talking about a light spritz, but a downright shower! He'll have to bathe in tomato juice to get rid of your smell. (For more on signature scents, please look at our *Parfum Exotique* chart in the Appendix. It's very important for an Other Rules girl to have a scent she's known by!)

Next, kiss his collar. We don't mean accidentally let your lips slide down there while he's wearing his shirt. No. Wait until he's in the shower, singing his heart out (show tunes are a bad sign, by the way), then go get his clothes and kiss all around his collar. Wearing your darkest red lipstick. The kind that won't come out. Ever.

Third, write a sexy note and stick it in his wallet. Where she's sure to find it if she goes through his things. (And you know she does, because you do.) Refer to specific parts of his anatomy in detail so that she knows you're not only fantasizing, you've visited his southern region. (In fact, it's your favorite vacationing spot.) If you have a photo of yourself that is flattering (of course you do!), stick it behind his driver's license. Caress it a little bit first so that it looks manhandled, as if he's been pulling it out at lunch and staring at it while he makes love to himself in the men's room.

To get truly down and dirty, pull several strands of hair from your head and lay them on his jacket lapel. This will only work if she has different-colored hair from you. If you have the same hair color as your enemy, pull some hair from one of your girlfriends' heads (make sure to tell her before you do this) and place it on his lapel. (Better yet, put it on his pillow if you can manage it.)

Make sure that during this war for his affections you leave plenty of messages on his answering machine. Always act as if you're calling him back, and make specific references to the times you two have spent together. The other woman will start to realize that whenever he says he's going out for milk, walking the dog, or visiting the gym, he really is with you!

It goes without saying that you should focus on what the two of you do between the sheets. Ask him to say your name as often as possible when you two make love. Soon he will begin to associate pleasure with your name. And sure enough, the next time he's with her, he'll moan your name instead of hers.

Bingo! You're the winner.

Rule 26
Woman Seeks Man—
Writing the Best Personal Ad

I would quite like to be the sexy man's think symbol.
—HELEN MIRREN

There was a time when personal advertisements got a bad rap. If you used one, you'd be considered desperate, and that's a word that makes an Other Rules girl shudder. But luckily this is no longer the case: Personal ads are the wave of the future. If you open up any hip newspaper or log onto the Internet and find a dating message board, you'll see column after column of people looking for love, sex, or both.

Some books will advise you to answer the personal ads yourself rather than placing your own. They say that this is the easier route because you won't have to put as much of yourself on the line. ("What if nobody answers your ad?" they say. "You'll be crushed!") But we don't agree with this advice. Of course men will respond to your ad! You're an Other Rules girl! And we want you to open your mailbox (or post office box) every day to an armload of letters, all from men who want to date *you*. What a great way to boost your ego, right?

To prepare for writing a successful personal ad, we believe you should get in the habit of watching late-night television. *Really*-late-night television. The stuff that comes on after the infomercial for the mop that cleans your ceiling. (Which you don't need, no matter how clever it looks, because you don't clean, remember?) You know you've got it when guys with slick hair and gold chains come on and tell you they're going to teach you how to get rich. Pay attention. You don't care about the money part of it—and no, you don't want to go out with them!—you want to know their method.

These guys say that the way to get the most response from an ad is to take out several small classifieds in your local paper. Keep refining them until you start to get answers. As soon as one of your ads begins to get you positive responses, start placing that same ad in newspapers around the country. If you can get just thirty positive responses per paper, and you've placed your ad in 30,000 papers, well, the mind literally boggles.

In all seriousness, there are several very important steps to writing a successful personal advertisement.

First you should learn the lingo. However, since

you're an Other Rules girl, you should also be prepared to improvise when necessary. Here are a few suggestions:

ACRONYM	TRANSLATION	OTHER RULES VERSION
ISO	In Search Of	I'll Sleep Over, I'm Slickly Oiled
VGL	Very Good-Looking	Very Gregarious Lesbian, Voluptuous Girl Lover
LTR	Long-Term Relationship	Looking to Romp, Loves to Rumble

Second, figure out how far you can go. Some newspapers reserve a special section in the Personals for, shall we say, "alternative" activities. In this section you may get very specific about your likes and dislikes, as well as the rest of your requirements. You may say that you want a man with leather pants and the body to fill them. You may say you're looking for a cave man or a guy with a big club. Whatever you want, they'll print, because your kind of ad makes more people pick up their newspaper. We strongly suggest you try this, even if just for fun.

Third, unless you must, don't ask for tall guys. Nothing in your ad should say "6' or over." This was suggested by Ann's brother, who is all of 5'6". He wants all you women out there to know that if you write "tall" in your personal ad, you will offend all vertically challenged men; he also wants to point out that height doesn't matter when you're horizontal. (He *made* us put this in. We happen to like 'em big and hunky.)

Fourth, decide where you stand on the oh-so-delicate issue of baldness. If his pate must have hair on it, say so in your ad. We won't stop you, and we understand. Some girls don't want to think about stocking up on Rogaine, and that's fine. But if you're willing to date bald or balding guys, you'll get many more responses. Moreover, these guys will probably be so grateful for the attention that they'll cater to your every whim. And you have many whims, don't you, girlfriend? Sure you do. Wouldn't you like them catered to? You bet. Plus, wouldn't you like him to excuse your foibles now and again, too? Think about it.

Rule 27
Don't Discuss *The Other Rules* With the Shrink You're Dating

I'm always running into people's unconscious.
— MARILYN MONROE

We know *The Rules* advises girls not to tell their therapists about its principles. As you may have noticed, we have very little in common with the writers of that book. In fact, we agree with just about nothing they suggest. But horror of horrors, we think they're on to something here. In one particular case, that is.

Let's say you're in therapy. (And please, please don't feel bad about it! Do whatever it takes to feel better about yourself, babycakes!) Let's imagine, just for fun, that you've noticed that your therapist is particularly attractive. In fact, were he not your therapist, you'd certainly be dating him. Well, here's what we say: Go on and date him! Why waste an opportunity? If he's making you feel pretty good just talking to you, imagine how good you'll feel once he starts doing other things!

But all will be for naught if he's on to you. You're entitled to a few secrets, after all. If you come right out and say to your shrink, "I'm using my Kitty-Cat Eyelash Bat on you," he'll naturally feel manipulated. And while you *are* going to manipulate your therapist, you don't want to let him to know about it, do you?

No way! By all means, play with your therapist's head like a kitten with a ball of string. Be deceitful. Tell sexy stories from your past that didn't actually happen to you. Come in sobbing and confess all of the dirtiest thoughts you've ever had. Try to include him if you can. If you prefer a more subtle approach, make up dreams rich with erotic symbols and watch him squirm as he reaches for an interpretation. See the chart below to help you do this:

DREAM SYMBOL	MEANINGS
Apple	Breasts
Bees	Aspirations of love
Being in prison	Sexual repression
Climbing stairs	Sexual intercourse
Creatures with horns	Male sexual potency
Doors	Bodily orifices
Fallen flower petals	Loss of virginity
Falling	Sexual intercourse
Fish	Male sexual urges

DREAM SYMBOL	MEANINGS
Gushing water	Orgasm
Hair	Sexual potency
Hats	Genitalia
Peaches	Female sex organs
Riding an elevator	Sexual intercourse

Sprinkle these symbols liberally through your dreams. For example, tell your therapist you've been having a recurrent dream about a hairy fish riding an elevator. Creatures with horns eating peaches while climbing stairs. Hat-wearing bees flying in and out of doors. Being in prison with water gushing and petals falling all over you. (Actually, that sounds a little cool to us.) Let your therapist decipher and decode them! Then pat the spot beside you on the couch and ask him if he wouldn't be a little more comfortable interpreting *from there*. We have a feeling he will move right on over and let you continue perfecting your repertoire of stares on him. And maybe, just maybe, he will give you one or two Eyelash Flutters back.

We won't tell if you don't!

Rule 28
Fed-Exing Your Panties and Other
Long-Distance Relationship Tips

Nothing risqué, nothing gained.
— ALEXANDER WOOLLCOTT

Let's say you're involved with some young hunk when suddenly he is transferred overseas. Or maybe you meet a stud at Club Med, but it turns out that he lives across the country from you. Or perhaps someone who answers one of your personal ads lives in Florida and can't come up with the cash to move to California to be with you.

We'll be honest. Long-distance relationships can be extremely trying. You can't win him over with your perfected stares; you can't keep him in line with your sexy walk. You can't chain him to your bed and leave him there until he's reformed from a lion to a pussycat (more on this in the Bonus Rules). But have no fear, sweet stuff, none of

this means that you, as an Other Rules girl, cannot make a
man want you from afar. Simply follow these guidelines
to a successful long-distance relationship:

• Get him off on the phone. As often as possible! If
you have daily phone sex with him you'll make it difficult for him to answer the phone without instantly
getting erect—sort of like Pavlov's dog. He'll start
getting hot whenever his phone rings, and he'll find
excuse after excuse to call you up. At work. On your
cellular phone. All the time.

Of course, if your man is really far away, you'll have
to budget your calls. When Ann's beau went to Russia
for three months, she wound up with $5,000 in long
distance bills. (Needless to say, that stripping job really
came in handy.) But if you don't want an unpleasant
surprise when you open your phone bill, watch your
time on the phone and follow the rules below....

• Get him off online. Make sure your man has a
computer, modem, and an online server. Then send him
the most erotic, explicit letters every day. Upload sensuous Polaroids of yourself (easy to take with a self-timer).
Photograph yourself in several stages of undress. (Hint:
If there is another guy in your pictures, have him
removed electronically! You can do this using different
computer programs currently available. Unless, of
course, the man you are seducing is into watching you
and another boy get it on. If this is the case, you can
always *add* a man into your pictures using those very
same computer programs.)

• Fed-Ex him a pair of your panties. Start with clean ones. We recommend choosing something to make his mind and body vibrate: a black lace thong. Stick a note in the Fed-Ex envelope. Describe how you tried on many different styles before you chose these. Explain in great detail how you and your best girlfriend camped out in a private dressing room at your favorite lingerie store and how she gave you advice on each and every item you tried. The velvet merry widow. The purple satin corset. The raunchy red underwire bra and matching red lace G-string. He'll be out of his mind fantasizing about what this scene was like. It doesn't matter if you got the panties from the 3-for-$5 bin at K-Mart weeks ago and haven't looked at them since. This is a case of giving the customer what he wants.

• Next, Fed-Ex him a pair of your, um, "used" panties. We don't mean that you should wear your underwear all day and send it to him. In fact, we didn't think you were actually wearing underwear all that often anymore. Here's what we mean: Pleasure yourself in your panties and send them to him. *Definitely* overnight them. You don't want your panties hanging out in a mailroom in Omaha.

By keeping your man busy with these activities, you'll know that you're satisfying him enough so that he won't turn to another girl while he's away from your loving arms. He'll be too busy rereading your erotic e-mail to his friends at lunch and downloading those photos you sent so that all the guys in his office can get a good look at you.

If you want to keep him even busier, ask him to return the favor. If he's kept entertained taking pictures of himself and trying to figure out how to make a pair of sticky boxer shorts seem sexy, he won't have the time to look at other women. Believe us.

We are confident that if you follow the Other Rules above, your long-distance man may cut short his trip (or move back to town) in record speed. If he doesn't, then simply enjoy the time that he's away. Taking pictures and Fed-Exing panties won't take you too long. In fact, it shouldn't cut into your dating time much at all. You can have a faraway boyfriend and a local one, too. Any man who truly loves you would want you to be satisfied, right?

Rule 29
The Other Rules of Adult Game-Playing

> You will do foolish things, but do them with
> enthusiasm.   —COLETTE

Guys like aggressive women. We hope you realize this by now. (If you don't, we advise you to start at the beginning and work your way through all the Other Rules again. It's the only way you'll learn!) Now we want to get specific. Guys will love you if you can beat them at any game. It will make their blood grow hot. Sure, they'll get defensive and demand rematch after rematch, but that's only because you've driven them wild with desire. Trust us: They're trying to figure out what you'll do to them in the bedroom if you can beat the pants off them in pool.

Some people will advise you to lose any game you

play with your man. We don't understand this concept. Why would we throw a game, be it Monopoly or basketball? We think that if you are going to be in an adult relationship, you should be in one with an adult. If your man turns out to be a big baby, dump him and find a guy who can handle being beaten by a girl!

Here are specific games that you should beat your man at:

• Pool: Have a pool shark teach you how to play. Once you understand the rules and can manhandle your way around a stick, practice the game while dressed to kill. We like wearing a low-cut black dress and extremely high heels. When you're really good, challenge your man to a game. Make sure you play in a crowded pool hall where people will start to make fun of him. This will get him all riled up for later, at your place, playing a different game entirely.

• Poker: Ask the guys at work to teach you when to hold them and when to fold them. Practice your poker face in the mirror until even *you* don't know when you're bluffing or not. When you feel in control of your hand (and your emotions), invite your man to play with you. Up the ante until he's wondering how he'll pay the rent next month. Win. Win again. Keep on winning until he starts to realize that losing to you is actually a good thing. (Note: If you don't want his money, play strip poker. When he's sitting across from you in his boxers and socks, let him win a round or two to make the night more exciting. Then move in for the kill.)

• Tennis: Take private lessons until you can cream all of your friends. Then invite your man to play with you. Beat him. When he wants a rematch, beat him again. When his face turns bright red and his ears look like they're going to explode, suggest he play you at a different game—perhaps a friendly game of football—and let him tackle you until he feels like you're even.

• Twister: This is a game with no losers. To experience the adult version, we recommend that you play it with your man naked and slathered in oil. If you're that kind of a girl, invite some of your friends to join you.

We promise that winning will get easier. And that the more you win, the easier you'll get.

Rule 30
Practice Makes Perfect

Wild oats will get sown some time and one of the arts of life is to sow them at the right time.
— RICHARD LE GALLIENNE

There. You're just about done. You've read the previous rules and you've thought to yourself: *Yes, yes, yes! I want to be an Other Rules girl!* But now you're in a bit of a quandary. How are you going to master the Other Rules and still handle the rest of the things you have going on in your life? You're a bright girl. You've got your job, the gym, and the nude modeling you do in your spare time. When are you going to fit the Other Rules into your busy schedule?

Well, dumpling, we'd like to be able to tell you that there's a secret for Other Rules success. We'd like to tell you that there are Cliff Notes, or clever ways to use crib sheets (just like you did in high school), but we'd be lying. And while lying to men is fine on occasion, we simply don't feel comfortable lying to you. Not after you were kind enough to buy our book.

But we do have advice that will help. (Don't we always?) If you want to be a successful Other Rules girl, you're going to have to practice, practice, practice. For example, we recommend that you walk around your apartment for a few weeks in your new heels before you try strutting your stuff in public. (Getting a heel caught in a subway grate and tripping is not something Other Rules girls ever want to do!) We suggest you practice lacing yourself into your new corset when you're all alone, rather than let him see you struggling to suck in your tummy. And we hope against hope that you'll try out your sexy "I Want You" voice on your girlfriends before you try it out on him.

We've heard some horror stories from friends who have half-heartedly practiced the Other Rules. They told us about blanking out on the Other Rules from time to time and actually doing the opposite of what we've been telling you. Big mistake! Let's say you stray from the Other Rules. For example, perhaps you find yourself turning down a date for Saturday when a man calls you after Wednesday. Maybe you let him (God forbid) pay for a meal. Try to forgive yourself, of course. These things happen, but you'll need to reread this book. Over and over again.

We never want you to get discouraged, however, if

you find yourself slipping. Keep right on practicing. Practice whenever and wherever and on whomever you can. Try the Other Rules on every man you meet. The mailman. The milkman. Your neighbor. The paper boy. Stare at them. Bat your lashes just like we taught you. Speak up and ask them out. Put on some funky music and ask them to dance. All of them. At once.

Pay attention to your wants and needs. If you want to call a man, call him. If you want to e-mail him, do it. If you lose your nerve, call up the other Other Rules girls in your support group (see the Appendix for more on this) and one of them will most definitely give you a kick where you most need it. Call a friend who is in the midst of having an amazing affair and let her fill you in on every single sordid detail. Talk to a married friend and have her describe her daily trials and tribulations. In moments, we assure you, you'll find yourself dolled up in heels and hose, ready to go out for a night on the town.

Yes, pretty soon, you're going to remember why the Other Rules are incredibly important. You'll start dreaming in rules. Rule 6 will dance before your eyes. Rule 12 will make appearance after appearance. Rule 7 will have you puckering up before he even arrives.

The most marvelous news, pet, is that the Other Rules are amazingly simple. And fun. So doing them won't be hard work. Simply remember to do them all the time. You never know when some guy will walk in and ask you to marry him. And then what will you do? If you haven't sown all of your wild oats—if you haven't dated Tom, Dick, and Harry—you'll be destined for a life of regret!

And if you ever do get married, The Other Rules will have given you a gift that no other self-help book could possibly offer. You'll have a plethora of remembrances that you can turn into a best-selling book of memoirs. Or maybe even a volume of women's erotica, which seems to be all the rage. Think about it. If you don't have any details to spill, there is little chance that you'll make it onto *The New York Times* best-seller list, which of course is where all of us want to be.

One last reminder: Please don't forget that the Other Rules are beneficial to your work life as well. Yes, you can practice the Other Rules while you're at your job. For example, if you have an adorable boss, by all means try out the Other Rules on him! Make sure he's aware of who you are, what you're capable of, and where your cubicle is located. Before long, we're sure he'll be dropping by and asking you to lunch. (Which, of course, you should pay for!)

If you consider *The Other Rules* your survival guide rather than simply a way to have more fun on the dating scene, you'll succeed beyond your wildest dreams. So buckle up tight and hold on. Dig in your spurs and keep your hands on the reins. You're in for a wild ride, sweetheart. A wild, wild ride.

Bonus Rules for Overachievers

These are for Other Rules gradu-
ates. Only after you've mastered
the Other Rules should you attempt these more advanced
rules! Otherwise we simply cannot take responsibility for
what might happen. For instance, if you haven't mastered
staring at men, and you try out the Eyelash Flutter on a
woman, you could wind up in a girl-girl relationship way
before you're ready for it! We don't want you to push
yourself, cupcake. Only do what feels comfortable to you!

That said, the following Other Rules deal with introducing your man to your sex toys, indulging in a lesbian
love affair, dating a transvestite, and more. So if you're
interested in exploring your wilder side, read on!

Rule 31
Revving His Engine—
When to Bring Out Your Sex Toys

There are two kinds of women: Those who want
power in the world, and those who want power in
bed.
          —JACQUELINE KENNEDY ONASSIS

We know all about that special
something that makes all
your dreams come true. Did you really think you could
hide it from us? Most likely it's a grade-A vibrator that
runs on double-C batteries. Admit it, you keep it well-
charged. (Your flashlight batteries may be dead, but this
emergency device is much more important!) But when
can you introduce your vibrator to your mate? And,
better still, how?

When is relative. If your man of the moment is going
to retain that status, you should bring out your toys on
the first date. In the first few minutes. Before he even
arrives. Arrange them attractively on your coffee table.

Show him everything you've got, from your lipstick-sized dildo to the vibrator that sounds like a Harley revving.

But what if you like this guy? *Really* like him. And you hope his car will be parking in your garage for the next few months? Then our advice is this: Tread slowly. You don't want to scare him off. Let him know that he is all-man, and that he is more than enough for you. Do this by pursing your lips in that baby-doll way that drives men crazy. Bat those pretty long lashes of yours. Moan and sigh each time he throws your legs over his shoulders.

When his ego is pumped fuller than a pair of ripe silicone breasts, the stage is set. Put on a skimpy outfit. Dim the lights. Pat the bed on your side and croon: "I've got a secret for you…"

Most likely, he'll say: "I like secrets." If he doesn't, nudge him a bit: "You like secrets, don't you?" If he has any sense, he'll nod that yes, he does.

Reach beneath the bed and pull out your favorite battery-operated lover. At first, your man will stall for time and feign confusion. He may even pretend not to know what your special device is. Be sympathetic. His mind is telling him: "I'm not enough for her. I knew it all along." But he won't want to believe it. So don't give him the chance! Say, "I adore everything we do, sweet-heart, but I thought we might play a little bit kinky tonight."

"Kinky" is your password to playtime, sister. For

most men, "kinky" makes everything all right. It gives them something they can snicker about as they huddle at the water cooler in the morning. ("And then she said she wanted to try something *kinky*….")

As his heart starts to beat at a rapid pace, and his eyes grow larger (along with another extremely important portion of his anatomy), lie back on the bed, spread your legs, and show him exactly what "kinky" means. Then hand over your favorite object and let him take a turn at the controls. When he sees how you respond, he'll probably want to join in. Let him! Try the toy on him, or keep pleasuring yourself while he moves into your normal routine. Pretty soon, he'll understand just why you like to keep this particular device close at hand. (And why you were in the dark during your last black-out.)

Maybe your favorite toy isn't battery-powered. Maybe it's an inflatable doll. A massage mitt. Lotion that gets hot when you blow on it. Nipple clamps. A video you've watched so many times you know all the words (and moans) by heart. Whatever it is that floats your boat, introduce it to your man in the sexiest possible way. Let him enjoy the item with you.

Then ask him to share his own favorite friend.

As long as she's inanimate.

Rule 32
Handcuffs "R" Us—Keeping Him Just Where You Want Him

A girl can wait for the right man to come along, but
in the meantime that still doesn't mean she can't
have a wonderful time with all the wrong ones.

—CHER

Do you have a man? A man worth keeping? If so, good. You've been following the Other Rules, and we're proud of you. But now you have a problem, you say? When you went out last, you noticed your man looking around. You caught him staring at the cute waitress at your local diner or making eyes at the receptionist at his office.

Okay, princess, it's time for you to take control. He needs to know who's boss—you. Yes, you.

Before you begin his training, it's time to do a little more shopping. Oooh! We just love going shopping! You're going to stride down to the nearest sexuality boutique and buy a pair of handcuffs. They can be the inexpensive type (about six bucks); just make sure they come with a key, and that it works.

The next time you find yourself in bed with your beau, which should be in about ten minutes or so if you're on an Other Rules schedule, mention that you have a surprise for him. Men love surprises. He'll get excited and look around the room and under the bed, hoping against hope that your surprise involves your best friend, Carly, or your nubile neighbor Korki. Look at him, the big lug. He has no idea what's about to happen! Tell him to close his eyes and you'll give him the surprise. Make sure he's not peeking! Then clamp one cuff around his left wrist, thread it through your curling brass headboard, and clamp the other cuff on his right wrist. (We told you the bed frame would come in handy.) Now watch his eyes bug out in surprise! It worked.

He may be squirming. He may demand that you take off the cuffs. Instead, make him enjoy being your sweet prisoner of love. Use your mouth, hands, and body until you've got him bucking and thrusting and begging all night! Or at least part of the night. For the rest of the time, punish him for looking at other women. Tell him you're on to his wandering ways. Let him know in no uncertain terms that you are not pleased with his behavior. We don't mean that you have to get our your quirt. We mean only that you should have a little fun without letting him join in.

If you're into a girl-girl scene, now's the time to

invite your cutest girlfriend over. Make out in front of your beau while he's chained and immobile. (You might want to make sure your bed frame can handle 200 pounds of straining pressure ahead of time. You do not want him to free himself on his own!)

If you don't feel up to a lesbian love affair, leave him cuffed to your bed while you pleasure yourself across the room. Put on one of your sexiest nighties—without panties, of course. Bring out one of your favorite sex toys. Seat yourself on a comfortable cushion or chair in full view of your man. And make yourself very, very happy. Don't move over to the bed until he begs you to. Really begs. Like the true puppy dog he is.

When you deign to join him on the bed, we promise you'll be in for a night to remember! He may even be sorry when you release him from the bed and let him free again. He may want to stay just where he is. If he does, we recommend that you let him. Because believe us, a man in handcuffs is yours for life!

Rule 33
Getting Him to Tie the Knot—
Exploring Your Submissive Side

Men play the game; women know the score.
—ROGER WODDIS

There was a time when even we didn't know how to ask for what we wanted. Really. We know we seem bossy and controlling now, but we were young once. (Or younger. We're still young, of course!) We were shy. Once we even drank a little too much wine and whispered to our boyfriend exactly what we wanted him to do to us. "Tie me up," we said. And he laughed! And hurt our feelings!

"The nerve!" you're yelling. (You'd better be yelling. We're having a very revealing moment here.)

After that, we didn't tell anyone. We went on date after date, hoping someone would catch on. Hoping someone would realize that we were experimental girls. That we

169

wanted to try a little bondage. Light bondage. No whips or chains or anything like that. We were simply interested in testing the waters. Seeing if it was for us.

Then we found a man who was willing, able, and more than ready to play it our way. By our rules. And we were in paradise. The benefits of experimentation are enormous. We trusted this guy. We let him tie our stockings around our wrists and bind our ankles to the bedposts with hair ribbons. We allowed him to pleasure us using his tongue in the most seductive, catlike way anyone has every imagined. And we discovered we loved it! Every moment of it! And that's codicil number two: When you start playing submissive games, find something that you like. If you experiment with bondage, but hate it, try something else. If you put on a blindfold, but don't like it, don't fret: There are plenty of other things you can do. Experimentation is the name and finding out what you like is the game!

Once you find activities that you enjoy, vary them. Sure, you love it when your man runs ostrich feathers along your naked, nubile body, but don't make him do it every time. He'll get bored playing fan boy to your Queen Nefertiti, and besides, his arm will start to hurt. Be creative! Play with manacles on Mondays, tickling on Tuesdays, water pistols on Wednesdays, tummy torture on Thursdays, fetish fun on Fridays, shrimping (a kind of toe-worship) on Saturdays, and just plain sex on Sundays.

Rule 34
Sex Party!— Introducing Your New Man to Your Friends

The love game is never called off on account of darkness.
—TOM MASSON

We know how it is. Sometimes you'll find it difficult introducing your new man to your pals. They can be jealous of the time you're spending away from them. Or jealous simply because you have a man and they don't. (If this is the case, please, please, buy them their own copy of *The Other Rules* so that they can have the happiness that you're finding! There are enough men to go around to make every girl happy!)

But if you've decided that your man-of-the-moment is going to be around longer than a night or two, then by all means introduce him to your gal pals. Some books will recommend moving slowly in this area. They

say that you should really get to know your guy before
you make the effort of sharing him around. We disagree
entirely. We say the more the merrier. Moreover, we
suggest that the best way to introduce your man to your
friends is to host a good, old-fashioned orgy, and make
him the *pièce de résistance*. This is the party for the '90s!

Of course, sex parties require a certain amount of
preparation. Here are a few tips we can vouch for
personally:

• Decide who you're going to invite. If you have a
lot of girlfriends, you'd better take care to invite a few
gentlemen callers, too. Do this by asking some of your
old beaux to come. That way, your man won't get too
much attention, and you won't end up having to pull
your girlfriends away from him at inopportune times.
Ask your girlfriends to bring along any stray men they
happen to know or meet along the way.

• Send out sexy invitations. You probably won't find
anything appropriate at your local Hallmark emporium,
so feel free to make your own. We generally put an
erotic drawing on the front, so people know what
they're getting into, and then list the important information inside. For example, if nudity is mandatory,
you're better off warning people in advance. If you don't
want to see anyone there gadding about in Nikes and
jeans, say so. You'd better tell people to bring cover-ups
in case of emergencies. What if there's a fire, or someone has to answer the doorbell? You don't want your
guests to freak out your neighbors, or your party may

end well before it's supposed to. And the police will not be amused.

• Plan your decorating scheme. For our sex parties, we simply spread cushions and comforters around the house and set up the mood lights. Of course, you can get fancier and develop a theme for the evening: Roman, Roaring '20s, Masquerade, and so on.

• Put out lots of condoms and other supplies. Your guests shouldn't have to bring their own.

• Set out board games for shy people: Boggle, Monopoly, and Sorry all seem to work well. Set these up in one room so you can dedicate the rest of the house to the free-for-all. Don't be surprised, however, if these games develop in interesting ways. Sex parties are contagious, and even the shyest among us seem to relax when they see others having a good time.

• Be sure to have on hand plenty of snacks and beverages. People can really work up an appetite during an evening of romping. Believe it or not, we like to serve pizza, quiche, sandwiches, and so on. In general we save our usual fare (pudding, tapioca, whipped cream) for our more private moments with a special partner.

One added note: Though you may be tempted to record the evening on film, we think sex parties are best left uncaptured by cameras, whether in videos or stills. Special evenings are usually all the more so when they are ephemeral. Besides, who's going to want to have to lug around a Camcorder on a night like this?

The Dyke of Your Dreams—
Attracting a Lesbian

> The sight of a beautiful woman has moved more
> lovers to madness than any other form of love.
> —*Vatsyayana Kama Sutra*

It's in the news. It's on TV.
Lesbianism is the way to go if
you're looking to be a hip chick. And we know you are.
Before you do anything else, turn off *Ellen*! Sure, you can
tape the episode and watch it later when you're done
reading this chapter, but we really don't want you to start
dressing like her. In fact, we'll never forgive ourselves if
you go outside dressed in her style! (What style?) Sure,
she's a lesbian, but so was Gertrude Stein and you don't
see any self-respecting dykes lining up to look like her!
Trust us, Ellen is funny, but she's not the girl you want
to mirror if you're looking to attract a pretty gay playmate. (If you don't believe us, believe Mr. Blackwell,
who just put Ellen on his worst-dressed list of 1997!)

Before you start choosing clothes, let's give your apartment the once-over. Do you have the proper CDs? We're talking Melissa Etheridge and kd lang (*of course*), plus the Indigo Girls, Tracy Chapman, Skunk Anansie, Nina Simone, Sarah McLaughlin, Ani Difranco, and anyone else who performed at the Michigan Women's Musical Festival or the Lilith festival. (No, they're not *all* lesbians, but most lesbians wish they were!)

Third, we need you to go to your nearest bookstore and purchase some cool lesbian literature. We're talking magazines: *Diva*, *Curve*, and *Girlfriends*. An issue of *Lambda Book Report* (if you want to appear bookish) and back issues of *On Our Backs* (if you want to appear sluttish) won't hurt either. Pick up a copy of the fabulous book *Oranges Are Not the Only Fruit* by Jeanette Winterson (or any other of her books, including *Sexing the Cherry* and *The Passion*), *Macho Sluts* by Pat Califia, *Bastard Out of Carolina* by Dorothy Allison, anything by Alice Walker, and the latest *Dykes to Watch Out For* by Alison Bechdel. Arrange them where your dates can see them. Flip through them if you have the time. While you're shopping, wander down to your local video store and purchase these movies: *Bound*, *Desert Hearts*, *French Twist*, *The Hunger*, *Heavenly Creatures*, and *Personal Best*. Line these up on top of your TV. Your girl will think you're extremely worldly, which never hurts!

Next, check your body to see if you have the proper piercings and tattoos. Maybe these seem passé to you, and maybe they *are* passé, but you can act as if you got them at the height of popularity and nobody will be any the wiser. (We promise not to tell!) Our favorite girl had a ring of barbed wire around her upper arm, a circle of roses around her ankle, and something exquisitely tribal on her lower back. Choose an icon that works (lotuses, calla lillies, and waterfalls are good), then make up a story about its meaning. Tread carefully: You don't want to appear superficial when your new girlfriend asks why you have an ankh on your ankle. Your answer should be something along the lines of: "The Egyptian meaning of the afterlife has always been important to me, blah, blah, blah…" Whatever you do, don't say: "Since my ankles are so slim and sexy, I thought that an adornment there would make girls want to lick them."

For piercings, the bellybutton is ever-popular. (That is, if you have a cute belly—if not, you haven't been following the Other Rules diet, have you? For shame! Turn immediately to the Appendix for help.) Also popular are tongue and nipple rings. If you don't want to be too extreme, get a couple of piercings in your ear and hang subtle silver hoops there. Your new friend will lick and pull them and drive you nearly crazy with want. (Earlobes are an oft-neglected erogenous zone. Trust us. We know!)

Now that you've come out of the closet, we'd like to explore it thoroughly. If you've been following the Other Rules, you've already outfitted yourself with many, many sexy outfits. Now you need to supplement your wardrobe with clothing that screams *lesbian*. We're talking tiny, tight T-shirts with funky, frisky sayings: I Can't Even Think Straight, Grrrl Power, Lucky Dyke, I'm Not Gay, But My Girlfriend Is, Femme, Girlie Girl, or Friend of Ellen's. All of these work very nicely and will get the point across. You should also own several pairs of Doc Martens (we like the red velvet and black patent leather ones) or engineer boots. Make sure you have overalls, long floral skirts, and a robe for yourself as well as one to loan out to your lover.

Remember when we told you that men don't make passes at girls who wear glasses? Well, we were telling you the truth. But we left out the fact that girls who like girls like girls who wear glasses. (Did you follow that?) Basically, if you get a pair of small, cute Lisa Loeb–looking glasses, the world will instantly know you're a dyke. If you don't need glasses, get some anyway. Put them on when you read, as if you're nearsighted. Or simply hang them from the neck of your T-shirt, as if you wear them sometimes, but not now. Better yet, indulge in neo-nerd chic and hang them from a beaded chain.

Let's go outside and look at your car. Do you have a rainbow sticker on the window or back bumper? Is your car sporting a pink triangle? If not, what in the world are you waiting for? While you're at it, why not add a bumper sticker that says, "Win a Toaster, Ask Me How." (Watchers of *Ellen* will understand. And giggle. And honk and wave when they drive by you.)

Now we need to ask you a very important question: Do you have a pet? If you don't, you should. We know we said to get rid of your cat way back when in Rule 1, but this does not pertain to lesbians. Girls like cats much more than boys do, and here is at least one of the reasons why lesbians should own feline (or at least furry) friends: Pets are great at helping you get dates! Say you see a possible playmate in line at the grocery store. You notice she's buying several cans of Sheba cat food. Well, honey, if you have a cat, there you go: conversation starter. Everyone knows she should be buying organic or making her own pet food.

If you're a dog person, pay attention when you walk your pooch at the park. While your puppy is sniffing benches and bushes, you should be on the lookout for any possible sniffee of your own! Finally, if you have a pet, you should buy cute food dishes, sweaters, and other accessories to match your *mode du jour*. For example, Hermès has a fabulous line of collars and leashes in six leathers and seventeen colors. At the very least, get your pet a rainbow collar. You should also stock up on an assortment of adorable squeaky pet toys: no boring chew bones for an Other Rules girl's Bowzer.

Speaking of toys, let's look at how you've outfitted yourself in that department. And believe us: If you want to bed a lesbian, it's key. Do you have a vibrator, dildo, and strap-on harness? Do you have lubricant, tasty lotions, body paints? No? Kiddo, what would you do without us? Head down to the nearest women's sexuality boutique, sister, and stock up! Right now! Times have changed: These stores are clean, attractively stocked, and

staffed by other women who won't make you feel embarrassed. At all. Pick up the biggest dildo you can find and
plunk down your money without shame. Try them all:
the Tongue, the Beaver, the Private Dancer. Even if you
don't use these playthings, having them around will make
you feel worldly, wicked, wild, and wanton. We should
warn you, however, that some lesbians do not like toys
shaped like a certain part of the male anatomy, and
maybe you yourself would rather have ones less realistic
in design. Don't worry, babycakes. Vibrators and dildoes
have been reconceived with girls like you in mind; they
now come in a wide variety of shapes, sizes, and colors.
Some look like little people. Some look like little
animals. Some just look a little weird. Find one that
appeals to you and stash it in a pretty toy chest.

It's time to discuss how to approach the object of
your womanly desire. Well, pumpkin, you're in for a
surprise! Do it exactly the way you'd approach an attractive man. The goal is the same, right? You want to bed
this person, and you want to bed her now! The only
difference is what goes on *in* the bedding! In case you
need a refresher, here we go. After making eye contact
over your compact, you realize that she is interested
from the way she gazes back at you. Slide, walk, or
dance closer and compliment her. Say you like her style.
Say you think she's angelic, devilish, or somewhere in
between. Make her feel wanted. This should be easy,
since you do want her.

When she slides her arm through yours, it's up to

you to keep up the conversation. You know how. You bought and read those magazines, right? And let's face it, they *were* pretty interesting. You should be reasonably up on lesbian topics; if you're not, just ask her questions about herself. Most people love to talk about themselves (straight and lesbian alike). We love to talk about ourselves. We can go on for hours....

Ooops! There we go again. By now, you and your honey are cozied up in front of the tube, watching *Xena*. We'll just leave you two alone.

Rule 36
Dressing for Excess—
Attracting a Transvestite

It's a good thing I was born a woman, or I'd have
been a drag queen.   —DOLLY PARTON

Okay, girls. Let's say the un-
thinkable has happened. You
come home early from work and can't find your boyfriend anywhere. You call out his name, but all you get
in response are muffled moans from the bedroom.
Quickly, you walk down the hall to your room, and lo
and behold, your boyfriend is parading in front of the
mirror wearing your undies. Your good undies! What
do you do now?

Do not panic! Simply because your man is wearing
women's underwear does not mean that he's not into
you. Some men simply get turned on by ladies' clothes
—but only when *they're* wearing them. These men find

something sexy in the satin or silk fabric, in the way the panties or dress feels on them. You can understand that, can't you? Wouldn't you rather wear girls' clothes than boys' clothes? Of course you would!

The first step in dealing with the situation is this: Calm down. Have a drink. (You can choose from the list of Other Rules girls' drinks in the Appendix.) Then talk to your boyfriend and broach the subject honestly. Is he dating you for you or for your clothing? Does he still want to be your boyfriend? Discuss the serious stuff and then either move on to a new beau or take this one out shopping with you!

Let's say you are interested in dating a transvestite —you aren't seeing one currently, but the thought appeals to you. We understand. We know how it is. Sometimes you just can't find a thing to wear. Your closet may be filled to brimming, but everything looks boring. If you want to double your wardrobe quickly, but don't have any spare cash, dating a cross-dresser is the way to go.

For some girls, transvestites are the perfect men. They like to shop. They actually care about how they look when they go out at night. No slouchy jeans or stained T-shirts for them! Plus, they take an interest in what *you* wear and will never ask you why you think you need another pair of shoes. They even let you borrow their razor to shave your legs—unless they're using it themselves. Basically, they understand what it means to be a lady.

Dating a cross-dresser can be fun! You'll put on makeup together and discuss the new cosmetics fads. Which blush is best for your skin tone? Is blue eye shadow really taboo? Does powder blush make your pores look enlarged? And you'll always have someone to turn to when you get a run in your stockings.

How can you attract a cross-dresser? It's as easy as pie when you're an Other Rules girl. You only need to do one thing: Accessorize! Wear your funky brocade vest with your gold embroidered handbag. Tie a chic scarf over your hair like Jackie O., and wear her signature sunglasses. Before you know it, a cross-dresser will have sidled up to you in size eleven pumps and asked you for your number. Or at least the number of your personal shopper.

There are some special things to watch for when dating a transvestite. First and foremost, be sure that you and your new man have similar tastes. If you're a retro girl and he's doing the '90s thing, it will never work, and we want to save you that heartache. It's better to stay home and watch QVC than bicker all night over the fact that his micro miniskirt doesn't look good with your new sandals. And if you find that you're at all territorial with your clothes, invest in a lock on your closet. A cross-dresser will not hesitate before helping himself to the darling little sweater you just picked up in Soho. (Even if you both know that leopard prints only accentuate his blotchy complexion!)

Smart Other Rules girls should also make sure that

they are dating a transvestite and not a transsexual. (We're talking post-operative, darling. Pre-ops are another story.) What's the difference? Transvestites still have all their manly parts and can do their duty in the bedroom. (In a stunning silk peignoir that matches yours!) Transsexuals should only be sought after if you are into the lesbian scene. (He may be a man inside a woman's body, but all of "his" plumbing is female.)

A final word of advice: When dating a transvestite, make sure he is not smaller or cuter than you! This happened to Julia, and was she miserable! Sharing a wardrobe is one thing, but it's something else entirely if he's got a tinier waist or better legs. There's nothing worse than dating a man who turns more heads in your favorite Calvin Klein slip dress than you do!

Appendix

Forming an Other Rules Support Group

*The trouble with some women is that they get all
excited about nothing—and then marry him.*
                                                    —CHER

You might think that practicing
the Other Rules is something
you should do on your own. Something you shouldn't
let any of your friends in on. After all, there's a man
shortage, isn't there? We don't agree, and we don't like
your negative thinking. We can think of several reasons
why you and your girlfriends should bond together and
create an Other Rules Support Group. And why you
should make sure each and every one of your girlfriends
has a copy of *The Other Rules*.

If you are following the Other Rules at the same
time as your friends, you'll be able to go shopping
together for items for your ABCs of sexy dressing. (You

can even share clothing, borrowing pieces when necessary!) You can practice walking in your new pumps, try out your sexy phone voices, or take turns doing your Kitty-Cat Eyelash Bats. You can discuss whether it's best to wrestle in pudding, tapioca, or whipped cream. You can get honest feedback about which hue of Saran Wrap looks best on you!

What if all of your friends are doing the Other Rules, and you find yourselves competing? Should you get new friends? No! Despite what you might think (or what you might have expected us to say), there are many more available guys than there are available friends. Instead, we advise you to create a support group with your Other Rules girlfriends and work things out. Divide up your town, neighborhood, office, gym, or whatever. Use a map. Highlight each girl's area with a different color. Yell "Dibs!" on a particular spot that you like. No cheating, in this case. You must play fair with your friends.

Once you have created a support group, make sure to use it. Sometimes you may simply want to get together with your girlfriends and dish on guys. Other times you might need a little extra help following the Other Rules. (Though we don't really know why. They're so easy!) Maybe you'll find yourself daydreaming about helping out with a soccer carpool, picking up some guy's dirty socks, or cooking up a skillet full of Hamburger Helper for three screaming rugrats. Let's say you start wishing you had a mother-in-law who liked to check in every day. If you find yourself having one of these down moments, your Other Rules Support Group can help.

In order to create a successful Other Rules support group, it's important to schedule, schedule, schedule. Find a time when all of your girlfriends can meet. We suggest lunchtime, since most of you will be busy every night. Choose a restaurant that serves a decent martini and order a pitcher of them. Then promise each other that if any of you, at any time, find yourself slipping, you can call each other for reassurance. Seal the bond with another round.

Your goal as support group sisters is to keep up each other's spirits. If a girl in your group asks out a guy and he turns her down, explain in no uncertain terms that the guy was probably gay, a loser, or in therapy. If one of you starts to date a guy exclusively, forgetting how many other cool guys there are out there, have an intervention. Grab her, tie her to a chair, and take turns discussing your sexual exploits. She's sure to see the error of her ways in no time. Or if, God forbid, one of your group gets engaged, plan her bachelorette party. Make it so absolutely fabulous that she will have to confront her decision to leave all the good stuff behind.

Be good to your Other Rules sisters. Go shopping together. Have makeovers. Go manhunting. And, whenever any of you needs an added lift, get together for a bit of girls-only socializing.

Of course, we are giving you each full approval to skip any support group meeting if you have a date. But that goes without saying, doesn't it?

Why Sex Is Better Than Chocolate—
The Aphrodisiacs Diet

Life itself is the proper binge.   —JULIA CHILD

Scientists, who conduct even more official studies than we do, have stated that chocolate releases the same endorphins in your brain that sex does. This explains why women like chocolate so much. But why bother with chocolate, we say? Why not simply have sex? You won't be gaining weight from all those Cadbury cream bars, Snickers, or Twixes (Twixi?), and you'll actually be burning off calories while those happy little endorphins fill your brain.

But didn't we promise you instant gratification back at the beginning of this book? Didn't we say that Other Rules girls do what they want, when they want, with whom they want? Yes, baby, yes. But we didn't really think you were going to *want* to sit in your bed in your jammies and eat chocolate instead of finding the hunk of your dreams. And even if that *is* what you want, we wonder why! If you practice the Aphrodisiacs Diet, you won't *need* your chocolate fix anymore: Your brain will be swimming with enough good-sex vibes to skyrocket your serotonin for life. Your body will be vibrating with orgasm after orgasm, and you'll be so proud of the slim, new you that you won't want marshmallow fudge cookies or Chunky Monkey ice cream.

Think back. Weren't you your thinnest during your best love affair? Didn't the thought of making whoopee kill the urge to stuff your face? Or are you one of those strange people who eats when they're happy? Get with the program, girlfriend! Most women eat when they're depressed, not blissful.

If you need other reasons to follow the Aphrodisiacs diet, we've listed them below:

• It's far easier to balance a cute, lithe, size-6 body on stilettos than it is to balance a pudgy one.

• If you eat chocolate before bed (up to *eight hours* before bed), it will keep you awake. If you have sex instead, you'll sleep like a baby!

• Eating chocolate burns hardly any calories. And, depending on how fast you can eat it, you're gaining an incredible amount of calories per minute. Having sex is an aerobic activity! Imagine how thin you'd be if you were making love all the time!

• When you finish eating a bar of chocolate, you probably feel guilty and beat yourself up for lack of willpower. When you finish having sex, you just lie there and sigh, luxuriating in the aftermath a dose of pleasure always brings. (Unless you're having sex with a married man, in which case you may have a twinge of guilt. But that will disappear in no time. We promise you!)

As with any weight-loss program, before you start this diet you should check your height to determine how much you should weigh. (Height is *with* heels, of course.) If you're naturally taller than 5'7", you should follow the common rule of starting with 100 pounds for 5', then adding five pounds per inch for each inch over. (Be sure you have your heels on. Even tall girls should wear at least 2" heels!)

Once you figure out how tall you are, compare your height with the height/weight charts available from any doctor or insurance salesman. Then smile, because there's just no way you're overweight! Feel better?

We must say (because our lawyers have demanded that we do) that we aren't dieticians or nutritionists: We don't have degrees in nutrition and we've never met Jenny Craig. We're just cute, slim women who get any man we want! So don't you want to trust us? Sure you do! Haven't you trusted countless other women just like us?

THE APHRODISIACS DIET

• Eat *only* aphrodisiacs. These include oysters, basil, honey, strawberries, coffee, rosemary, and figs. (Sure, some scientists say that none of these foods really affects the libido, but what do they know?) If you only eat the foods listed above, you're sure to lose weight. And if you mix them up and serve them together, we're pretty sure you'll lose your appetite completely!

• When you go to a restaurant, have sex rather than dinner. Try it in the bathroom or out in the parking lot. Reach under the table and grope each other while you sip your wine.

• Only eat peeled grapes. Have him peel them for you. This takes a lot of effort, and we're sure he'll get tired after a few minutes. So you won't really consume much food at all.

• Instead of going out for lunch, cab over to his office and do it on his desk. (Lock the doors and keep your voices down! Unless he's the boss, in which you can do just about whatever you like and no one will dare say anything about it!)

• Don't drink the champagne he's brought to your place: Take a bath in it. (Of course you can have a little. It's a bit difficult not to get some in your mouth when you're sliding about underwater. But you'll have more fun floating in those bubbles than slurping them down. Plus, you won't have nearly as bad a headache in the morning.)

• The next time you're inclined to share a pint of super-fat deluxe ice cream with your beloved, *wrestle* in it instead. Wrestling burns off a lot of calories. And we're betting you're not going to be interested in eating what's left over!

• Switch to low-calorie whipped cream for your whipped-cream fights.

Follow these rules and you'll be a slender nymphet in no time. We promise! This diet has worked for us for years! If you must have your chocolate fix, give in. It's okay to indulge yourself from time to time. Why not try licking it off him, though? That way, you'll get your man and your Godiva truffles too—which, according to some of the girls we know, is the best of both possible worlds.

"I'd Like a Cocktail…"—What Other Rules Girls Drink (With Recipes!)

One more drink, and I'd have been under the host.
— DOROTHY PARKER

All true Other Rules girls have their own special drinks. That way, they look sophisticated, like James Bond—who always orders a very dry martini, shaken, not stirred. Now's your turn to choose a drink that best suits you, your mood, and your personality!

ANGEL'S KISS
Crème de cacao
Heavy cream
Fill 3/4 of a liqueur glass with the liqueur. Add a dollop of cream.

CORKSCREW
1 1/2 oz. light rum
1/2 oz. dry vermouth
1/2 oz. peach liqueur
Shake well. Strain into chilled glass. Add a slice of lime.

CUPID COCKTAIL
2 oz. sherry
1 fresh egg
1 tsp. powdered sugar
1 dash cayenne pepper
Shake well. Strain into glass.

DEVIL'S TAIL
1 1/2 oz. golden rum
1 oz. vodka
1/2 oz. lime juice
1/4 oz. grenadine
1/4 oz. apricot liqueur
Shake well. Strain into glass filled with crushed ice.
Add lime slice.

MAIDEN'S BLUSH
Curaçao
1 dash lemon juice
4 dashes orange
4 dashes grenadine
1 1/2 oz. dry gin
Shake well. Strain into glass.

SCREWDRIVER
1 1/2 oz. vodka
4 1/2 oz. orange juice
1 tsp. lemon juice
Pour over ice cubes.

SHERRY FLIP
1 tsp. sugar
1 whole egg
1–2 oz. sherry
nutmeg
Shake well with cracked ice.
Strain into cocktail glass.
Top with nutmeg.

TEQUILA BODY SHOTS
Tequila
This isn't really a cocktail, but we like it just the same.
Order a shot of tequila. Have your man sprinkle salt
on his hand and hold a lime in his mouth, pulp-side
out. Do your shot, lick his hand, and then suck the
lime from his lips. *Voilà!*

Updating Your Personal Library

Books are no substitute for living, but they can add immeasurably to its richness.
—MARY HILL ARBUTHNOT

We're guessing you have a bookshelf in your bedroom. Or at least a nightstand piled high with the mysteries, memoirs, romance novels, and fashion magazines you spend your few free moments perusing. Below is a list of titles you should have on display (and a few others you should give away).

BOOKS FOR YOUR SHELF
The Guide to Erotic Massage
Delta of Venus by Anaïs Nin
Anything by Anne Rice
The Illustrated Kama Sutra
120 Days of Sodom
Sensuous Magic
How to Please Your Man in Bed
The Lusty Lady
Story of O
Spanking the Maid
Lady Chatterley's Lover
The Joy of Sex

BOOKS TO GIVE AWAY
The Girlfriends' Guide to Pregnancy
Anything by Gloria Steinem
The Courage to Heal
Planning Your Wedding
The Celibacy Club
1,001 Baby Names
One Hundred Years of Solitude
Our Bodies, Ourselves
Understanding Feline Behavior
Dog Love
When I Say No, I Feel Guilty
The Rules
The Rules II

The Other Rules Video Collection

I think it's quite nice that people have seen my
snatch in their living rooms, or wherever, especially when they're never likely to see it for real.
—TUPPY OWENS

On top of your TV, make sure
you have at least three of the
following videos. (Note: for a movie to be in your
collection, all it really needs to have is a sexy title. The
actual film could be about anything, but if it sounds
good, use it!)

VIDEOS FOR YOUR COLLECTION

After Dark, My Sweet

An Affair to Remember

Basic Instinct

*Best Little Whorehouse
  in Texas*

Body Heat

Choose Me

Dangerous Liaisons

Dirty Dancing

*Doña Flor and
  Her Two Husbands*

Earth Girls Are Easy

Easy Rider

Exotica

A Few Good Men

Flashdance

French Kiss

Going My Way

Grease

It Takes Two

The Lady and the Tramp

The Last Seduction

Let's Do It Again

Little Foxes

The Long Kiss Goodnight

Long, Hot Summer

Love at First Bite

Love Me Or Leave Me

Love With the Proper Stranger

The Lover

Madame X

*Mama, There's a Man
  in My Bed*

Ménage

Moby Dick

9 1/2 Weeks

Obsessed

A Piece of the Action

The Player

Private Parts

The Professional

The Right Stuff

Same Time Next Year

Satisfaction

Sex, Lies, and Videotape

She's Gotta Have It

Showgirls

Some Like It Hot

Something Wild

The Sure Thing

Swing It, Sailor

Swingers

Tickle Me

Tie Me Up, Tie Me Down

Under the Yum Yum Tree

<u>HIDE THE FOLLOWING VIDEOS IMMEDIATELY</u>

Baby Boom

Bride of Frankenstein

Bringing Up Baby

Clueless

Diary of a Mad Housewife

Easy to Wed

Fatal Attraction

Father of the Bride

First Wives Club

Four Weddings and a Funeral

Heartbreak Ridge

How to Marry a Millionaire

I Love Trouble

I'm Gonna Get You, Sucka

The Incredible
   Shrinking Man

The Innocents

Maybe, Maybe Not

Mr. Wrong

Much Ado About Nothing

Muriel's Wedding

My Best Friend's Wedding

Never on Sunday

Never Talk to Strangers

Nine Months

No Way Out

Outbreak

Parenthood

Presumed Innocent

Pretty Baby

Pretty in Pink

Sense and Sensibility

Seven Brides
   for Seven Brothers

She's Having a Baby

Sleeping With the Enemy

Snow White

Suspicion

The Taming of the Shrew

Terms of Endearment

Thelma and Louise

Too Beautiful for You

The Untouchables

The Wedding Banquet

Woman Under the Influence

Women on the Verge
   of a Nervous Breakdown

Parfum Exotique— Choosing Your Signature Scent

For me, a woman who wears no perfume has no future.
—PAUL VALERY

Other Rules girls most definitely wear a signature scent. They spray it in their hair, on their clothes, on their boyfriends' clothes, and so on. Now's the time for you to choose yours. We've listed several below that we think you might find apropos.

Pick-a-Perfume Chart

Perfume	Maker	Reason
Beautiful	Estee Lauder	You get to say you're wearing it; he gets to say it suits you.
Contradiction	Calvin Klein	Men like complicated women, don't they?
Curve	Liz Claiborne	You'll throw him for one, that's for sure.
Dolce Vita	Christian Dior	It means "sweet life," which is what you have.
Egoïste	Chanel	Sticks and stones may break our bones, but....
Envy	Gucci	What you'd like to inspire.
Knowing	Estee Lauder	Of course you are.
Obsession	Calvin Klein	Stinks up a room in no time; he'll remember you for days.
Poison	Christian Dior	Perfect heartbreaker perfume.
XS	Paco Rabanne	As extreme as you feel.
212	Caroline Herrera	A notch here, a notch there, and soon you'll be up to this many, at least.

We advise you to choose a scent that you not only like to smell (and smell like), but also like to say. Practice saying the name of it in the mirror. When some adorable man in the elevator asks you what you're wearing, you'll be able to smile, wink (just like we taught you), and whisper, "Obsession...."

By the way, Other Rules girls never wear Dune, Sunflowers, or White Linen. Ever.

Hint: If his ex-girlfriend wore your fragrance, change it. You don't need to be reminding him of anyone else. You want to create brand-new memories starring you and you alone. (Or you and your cutest girlfriend. But that's it!)

Choosing Your Theme Song

Lay, lady, lay. Lay across my big brass bed.
— BOB DYLAN

You may have noticed in movies that stars will be given a theme song. And whenever there is an important scene, that music plays in the background. On television, the show's theme song becomes the star's theme song. If the star wins an award, that music is played while he or she walks up to the podium to be congratulated.

In our humble (well, not so humble) opinion, we believe that Other Rules girls should also have theme songs. We don't expect you to play these songs while you're walking down the street, but you can hum them or sing them softly to yourself if you have a nice voice.

Following are some of our personal favorites:

Song	Artist
"Cream"	Prince & the NPG
"Doin' It"	LL Cool J
"Express Yourself"	Madonna
"Girls Just Wanna Have Fun"	Cindy Lauper
"Handy Man"	Alberta Hunter
"I Got a Man"	Positive K
"I Want Your Sex"	George Michael
"I'm Too Sexy for My Clothes"	Right Said Fred
"In the Mood"	Glenn Miller
"Love in an Elevator"	Aerosmith
"Need You Tonight'	INXS
"Simply Irresistible"	Robert Palmer
"Something to Talk About"	Bonnie Raitt
"Squeeze Box"	The Who
"Sweet Thing "	Van Morrison
"Why Don't We Do It in the Road"	The Beatles
"Whatever Makes Baby Feel Good"	Parliament
"Wicked Game"	Chris Isaak
"Wild Thing"	Sister Carol
"You Got Me Rocking"	Rolling Stones

SONGS THAT OTHER RULES GIRLS NEVER PICK

"Beloved Wife"	Natalie Merchant
"Bye Bye Baby"	Madonna
"Fifty Ways to Leave Your Lover"	Paul Simon
"I Can't Be With You"	The Cranberries
"I'm a Mother"	Pretenders
"I Wonder Where Our Love Has Gone"	Ella Fitzgerald
"Loser"	Beck
"Love and Marriage"	Frank Sinatra
"My Lovin' (You're Never Gonna Get It)"	En Vogue
"Somebody's Gettin' on My Nerves"	Salt-n-Pepa
"Sullen Girl"	Fiona Apple

Meet the Authors

Ann Blakely and Julia Moore are best friends who live in Northern California.

They put the Other Rules into practice on a daily basis. Needless to say, they couldn't be happier.

They would like to thank Richard Kasak, Marti Hohmann, Jennifer Reut, Alana Lesiger, Champagne Sam, Sue Landers, and Fifi for all their hard work and incredible support on this project.